D0773250

Who
Talked to the President
Last?

By Will Sparks

Drawings by J. Vinton Lawrence

Who Talked to the President Last?

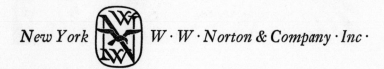

New York W · W · Norton & Company · Inc ·

Library of Congress Catalog Card No. 70-137883
SBN 393 08626 7
1 2 3 4 5 6 7 8 9 0

This book is dedicated to my wife, Zona, who refrained from laughing for five years while I took all this seriously.

Contents

Humor is the only test of gravity, and gravity of humor, for a subject which will not bear raillery is suspicious, and a jest which will not bear serious examination is false wit.

—ARISTOTLE, *Rhetoric*

Introduction

"NO MAN EVER SAW A GOVERNMENT," said Woodrow Wilson. "I live in the midst of the Government of the United States, but I never saw the Government of the United States."

I, too, once lived in the midst of the Government of the United States and may have been more fortunate than President Wilson. There were moments when I thought that I had actually caught a glimpse of it. Certainly I have seen the footprints it left while walking through the White House rose garden.

Whether the Government of the United States really exists, whether it can be seen, felt, or tasted is, however, one of the many important questions not answered in the following pages. This is not a book about the government. It concerns certain kinds of people who, whatever the government may be or wherever it may be located, are convinced that they run it. All the individuals we are about to meet suffer this delusion, with the possible exception of the President himself. Thanks to the Constitution and the vagaries of politics, this mental aberration is mercifully temporary—there being, under our system of government, no such thing as a permanent White House pass.

Let us count our blessings.

My first encounter with Washington occurred not long after my first experience with sex. Perhaps for the same reason. During the acute manpower shortage of the Second World War, while still in my teens, I became Assistant to the Editorial Director of the Department of Information of the Office of Price Administration.

Since rank or status in government is inversely proportional to the length of one's title, I obviously did not start at the top. A wise man learns from the mistakes of others, however, and so the careful student of this little handbook should be able to avoid my misfortunes.

My principal memory of OPA concerns a day—possibly the only day—when I got to the office before anyone else. I answered an urgently-ringing telephone on my boss's desk and there ensued the following dialogue:

Caller: "This is Steve Early's office."

Sparks: "Steve *who?*"

Caller: "Steve Early *at the White House.* Your *bill* is ready."

Steve Early, of course, was FDR's press secretary. Now, brave and famous heroes have been known to retreat into dumbfounded silence upon their first unexpected call from the White House. It is different with those of us who are born with a natural aptitude for government. The conversation continued:

Sparks: "*Our bill?* What bill might that be?"

Caller: (*With mounting incredulity*) "Your *appropriation* bill—the bill that pays your salary for another year!"

Sparks: (*Calmly*) "That's wonderful. I didn't know we were broke but I'm sure everybody will be glad to hear we're still in business. I'll tell them as soon as they come in."

And I hung up. On the White House.

A short time later, I left Washington and returned to college. I was not yet old enough to vote, and my government career seemed already behind me. Perhaps it should have stayed that way. But because God is just and believes in balancing his accounts, however slowly, I was returned to Washington some two decades later so that I might sit at 1600 Pennsylvania Avenue and have that same conversation several thousand times, from the other end of the line.

Like most citizens, I had over the years frequent contacts with representatives of our federal government. Conversations with ladies and gentlemen from the Internal Revenue Service. Discussions with officials of the Defense Department about when, if ever, I might expect to be paid for work performed under a government contract. Welcome-home greetings from the Customs and Immigration Service after trips abroad. And, on more than one occasion, a timely lecture by a Foreign Service Officer in one of our embassies about why the State Department could not afford to get involved with my personal problems. (These lectures, incidentally, are always cordial and given without regard to place or person; Presidents of the United States often get similar advice from the very same people within the walls of the White House itself.)

Thus, long before meeting a cabinet officer or setting foot in the White House, I acquired real admiration for those described in Article Two of the Constitution as the "inferior officers" of government. Or, as we know them today, our career civil servants.

Theologians tell us that a man's lifetime is but the tick of a second in the halls of the Almighty. So it is also in the corridors of government. To the true civil servant, time's basic unit is thirty years—the normal span between his first assignment and the pleasures of retirement. This is one reason why, as a rule, nothing is ever done in Washington (not to mention London, Rome, or Moscow) until it has needed doing for so long that it is really time to be doing something else.

The career official is not to be censured for his attitude, which is, in any event, inevitable. While it may be frustrating to those who, like most Presidents, want desperately to remake the world during their few days of power, the genial placidity of the career civil servant may also have saved us from numberless evils we know not of—every decision having at least a fifty percent chance of being wrong.

For good or ill, the senior civil servant is like a great granite rock deposited in the middle of a lake carved by some long-vanished glacier. He never makes waves, but watches with cool detachment as each new administration

comes pouring in like a mountain stream during the spring thaw, swirls about for a time, muddying the waters, and then trickles quietly down to the sea of oblivion.

This little volume is not for him. The career official can accept with biblical resignation the slings and arrows of successive generations of political appointees because he knows with perfect certainty that this, too, shall pass. If he appears at all in these pages, it is because we have stolen here and there some small portion of his accumulated wisdom to share with those May flies of government of whom I was once one: the presidential appointees, the cabinet officers, the under-secretaries, the bright young men, the speech writers, the aides and assistants who seem to spring from nowhere and for one brief day are allowed to fling themselves against the windows of the White House, obscuring the view.

A word about the organization of this book. For the convenience of the serious student, I have tried to arrange the principal topics, maxims, and guidelines under chapter headings which will lead you quickly to the material you need most urgently. If you have just been nominated to the cabinet, for example, you should turn directly to the chapter on cabinet officers—preferably while there is still time to change your mind.

That emergency past, you would be well advised to study the book in its entirety. At the very least, you will want to peruse the chapter on "special assistants." You will be surrounded by many of these young men—unless, as sometimes happens, an especially brilliant practitioner has managed to reduce the field to one survivor, himself. They (or he) will have the combination to your safe, your unlisted phone number, your confidence, and the cloak of your authority. Unless you want one of them to end up with your job and maybe your wife, you should learn as much as possible about how they operate.

Finally, if you have any reason to believe that you are, or are about to become, President of the United States, I respectfully suggest, Sir, that this book is virtually required reading. After a year or two in office, I believe you will agree that much of American history might have been different if your distinguished predecessors had been adequately alerted to the phenomena described in these pages.

Knowing what we know now, would President Monroe have been foolish enough to sign the Tenure of Office Act in 1820? You will recall, Mr. President, that this was the law limiting all government officials to a four-year term, after which they had to be reappointed by the President, or go home. Former Presidents Jefferson and Madison warned President Monroe that he was making a crazy mistake. Jefferson told him that he would only manage "to keep all the hungry cormorants for office in constant excitement." But President Monroe didn't listen, possibly because he didn't know what a cormorant was, and we got fifty years of chaos which moved President Lincoln to complain: "If ever this free people—if this government itself is ever utterly demoralized, it will come from this incessant human wriggle and struggle for office, which is but a way to live without work."

Mr. President, you and anyone else who reads this book will *know* what a cormorant is.

I hope it helps.

Who
Talked to the President
Last?

I

The Art of Being Honorable

Titles of honor and dignity once acquired in a democracy, even by accident and properly usable for only forty-eight hours, are as permanent here as eternity is in heaven.   —MARK TWAIN

OUT IN THE Southwest some years ago there occurred one of those lawsuits for damages which are the mainstay of our legal profession. A civil lawsuit is for the lawyer what the annual checkup is for your family doctor: it keeps him in practice until you really need him.

In this particular case, the defendant was represented by an attorney who had once been a high-ranking Washington official. The chief witness for the plaintiff was a local cattle auctioneer whose status in the community was roughly equal to that of a Medici moneylender in the Golden Age of Venice. He was, naturally, a Kentucky Colonel.

After hours of vain effort to poke a hole in the Colonel's testimony, the frustrated lawyer made a foolish attempt to disparage the witness's reputation.

"Isn't it true," he demanded, "that the word 'Colonel' in front of your name is purely honorary? That you did nothing whatsoever to earn it? That it means absolutely nothing?"

"That is correct, Sir," responded the witness. "The word 'Colonel' in front of my name means about as much as the word 'Honorable' in front of yours."

Such cynicism notwithstanding, you will find that being addressed as "The Honorable" is one of the few lifelong advantages accruing to you as a reward for serving your country. Tradition and protocol dictate that judges, members of the Congress, Presidential appointees, and certain others remain Honorable for the rest of their lives. Indeed, there have been Congressmen who, through some unfortunate misunderstanding, have climaxed their political careers with long visits to outposts of the Federal Bureau of Prisons and who yet continue to call themselves The Honorable. It is a tradition derived from our English heritage. No matter what hardship or decadence fate may bring you —once a gentleman, always a gentleman.

While you remain in office, this honorarium will also help to distinguish you from the three million career employees of the Civil Service—those "inferior officers" of the Constitution—who don't get to use the title. (A career Foreign Service Officer who rises to the rank of Ambassador is sometimes referred to as "His Excellency," but this is a separate situation which you can and should ignore.)

You will have many other advantages. But, to quote a venerable military axiom, "Rank hath its privileges—and so hath its troubles." To begin with, you will have to make the painful transition from private to public life—a trip once described by George E. Allen, after his appointment to the Reconstruction Finance Corporation by President Truman, in these words:

"If I had ever entertained any illusions about my character and capacities (and I had), they were now stripped from me by the columnists and commentators. I became a man possessed of neither integrity nor intelligence. I became a scandal. It is a strange sensation, being a public scandal. I read the columns and I began to be outraged myself at this ridiculous appointment of a man without a vestige of qualification for the job. It was difficult to remember at times that they were talking about me, George Allen, a fellow for whom I personally had the highest regard."

Having paid the price for your title, there are certain guidelines you will be expected to follow in return for the honors and prestige heaped upon you by a grateful nation. Here are a few primary directives which apply to all Honorable Men, regardless of duties or title.

You Must Work Long Hours. There are 168 hours in a week. You should make every effort to spend as many of them as possible in your office. An eighty-hour work week is excellent; seventy hours is acceptable; less than seventy is dereliction of duty and will ultimately destroy you. In this respect, at least, the working conditions of appointed officials have changed considerably since President Lincoln's day.

You should maintain this schedule for many compelling reasons. First there is the fact that all employees of the Executive Branch, under the Constitution, work for the President of the United States. At least such is the theory, and Presidents have a wistful way of hoping to see theory reflected in practice. Since in this era Presidents of the United States *must* work at least eighty hours a week just keeping their backs to the wall, they have an understandable tendency to look with suspicion on people who go home at five o'clock.

Beyond that, you will also enhance your moral superiority over the career employees, who, with their eyes fixed on that magical thirty-year mark at the end of the road, will wisely refuse to shorten their lives to promote the foolish enthusiasms of your administration.

There would be nothing for them to do, anyhow, because work done at midnight in government offices almost always concerns activities designated as "closely-held," which really means, "Don't let anybody else see this except One of Us because it could be Political Dynamite in the hands of the Opposition."

Many senior career civil servants have a direct line to key members of the Congress and can be depended upon to make sure that any such information does indeed get into the hands of the Opposition. Sometimes this is a device to head off an administration program the career man honestly believes to be ill advised; more often it is his personal insurance for survival in case your party loses the next election.

A recent American Secretary of State once told the

British Foreign Minister how much he admired the English Civil Service. Because, he said, it always loyally supports the party in office regardless of personal convictions.

"Not at all," said the Minister. "It has nothing to do with convictions. It's just that *our* civil servants think it poor manners to support more than one party at a time."

An important part of the Art of Being Honorable is never forgetting that our own people have not developed this sense of propriety. Controlling the career staff in your domain will require constant effort and many talents, none of which will avail you aught, however, if you do not begin by outworking them. Let your motto be *"Anything you can do, I can do longer than you."*

The need for spending long hours in the office has no necessary connection with the number or nature of your responsibilities. Dean Rusk once suggested that the reason for late hours in government offices is simply that the earth is round. Only one-third of the human race is asleep at any given moment. The other two-thirds is awake—and usually up to some kind of mischief.

That may explain it for the State Department, but what about the Department of Housing and Urban Development? With all due respect to Mr. Rusk, I suggest that the real secret lies elsewhere. The real reason for marathon hours as a *routine* is that government is essentially unproductive.

In one significant aspect Washington resembles Wall Street; both are in the business of putting words and numbers on pieces of paper. There is also a profound difference: Wall Street's paper consists of stocks and bonds which can be (sometimes) sold for a profit.

Washington prints money of course, but the money leaves almost immediately for New York.

Washington also writes tax laws which eventually bring most of the money home again.

But, except for those who work for the Bureau of Engraving and Printing, or the Internal Revenue Service, everybody in Washington is engaged essentially in producing memoranda. If a Wall Street underwriter issues a new stock priced at $10 a share and the Public (the same name, incidentally, by which this mysterious group is known in Washington) shows a willingness to buy it for $40 a share two hours later, the underwriter goes home knowing that at the very least he has saved his children from public school for one more year. He has accomplished something. But what has the government memo writer achieved? How much is a government memo worth? Where is the market place where the devisor of new values can establish a fair price for his most recent effort?

There is only one solution: you must be the hardest-working man in the office. You may not be able to tell anyone what you are doing. You may not even *know* what you are doing. What you are doing may be bad for the country. You can nevertheless demonstrate that, whatever your thing is, you are doing it with outstanding dedication.

Being the first in and last out of the office need not reduce you to a monastic existence if you will only learn a few harmless ruses. At lunchtime, it is never hard to find an excuse for visiting some member of the White House staff, and the White House is within walking distance of some of Washington's better restaurants. The aide may even be glad to join you, since liquor is served in the White House staff mess only on very special occasions, and sometimes not then. You may be confident that nobody from your office will ever page you at a meeting in the White House—unless you have instructed them to do so, which is part of another game.

You might follow lunch with a visit to the Pentagon—always impressive—where, if you have made the right friends, you can use the pool, the steam room, and the squash courts in the officers' club. (If you happen to be the Secretary of Defense you can do all this without bothering to make friends, which is extremely fortunate, considering your situation.)

In the evening, you may definitely go to cocktail parties. Going to Washington cocktail parties, for a high-ranking American official or a spy in the employ of a foreign power, is part of your job description. You can turn these recreations to additional advantage by adopting the strategy invented by one cabinet officer who made a point of always arriving early, staying until most of the other guests had arrived, several drinks later, and then departing with the apology that he "had to get back to the office."

What you must avoid at all cost is attending any Washington social event out of genuine pleasure. The moment you find yourself actually enjoying a Georgetown cocktail party it is time to get out of the District of Columbia and go back to where you came from. Like Hollywood, Washington is a company town in which the mill owners live on top of the hill, the superintendents a little farther down the slope, and everyone else down in the valley. One does not attend a Washington social affair for the purpose of *being* there; one goes for the purpose of *having been*. This is harder than it sounds. There are usually more people at a White House dinner, for example, than are listed on the official guest list. But it is the official list that is printed next morning in the *Washington Post*. The unlisted and unsung might just as well have stayed home and spared themselves the speeches.

2

How to Hide in the Cabinet

Cabinet: a little cabin, hut, soldier's tent; a rustic cottage; a lodging, tabernacle; a den of a beast.   —*The Shorter Oxford English Dictionary*

THE *Government Organization Manual* tells us that, after the President, the most important people in Washington are the members of his cabinet. This is as good an excuse as any for dealing with them first. It is even occasionally true.

Political scientists have defined politics as "the art of who gets what, why, and how." Among the prized rewards for being a member of the winning team in American politics is a seat in the cabinet. It is of passing interest that in modern times, at least, almost no one has volunteered to be so honored twice.

If you *will* be a cabinet officer, at least try to start on the right foot. The most important decision you will make as a cabinet officer will be made long before you arrive in the office to take charge of your department or even before you reach Washington.

You must decide why the President gave you the job.

In making the appointment, the President will say that after a nationwide talent search he has found exactly the right man for the job. The President is delighted and deeply grateful that you have consented to serve, at great personal sacrifice, in this most exacting office. Indeed, the President believes, in these trying times yours may prove to be the most critical cabinet post of his administration.

Since the President makes this same speech every time he appoints a new cabinet officer, nobody believes it, least of all the President. (President Nixon initiated the custom of introducing all of his cabinet in the same ceremony, thus covering everyone with the same speech. But the principle is unchanged.) It is your responsibility to provide the press and the public with some plausible reason for your elevation to the cabinet.

Remember, this is a critical decision. The image you choose for yourself at this moment will be the standard by which you will be judged during your entire Washington career. Pick one you can live up to, or at least with.

You know, of course, that you were tapped for this job through a chain of accidents so extraordinary that the most sophisticated computer could not have predicted it. Such awareness may tempt you, if you are emotionally mature and basically honest, to tell God's own truth to the first reporter who asks why the President appointed you.

You may want to say, "I have no idea"; or "I guess he couldn't find anyone else foolish enough to take the job"; or even "I was sick of what I'd been doing and this looked like a good change of pace, so I talked him into it."

Those are honest answers which would lay up treasure

in heaven for anyone. But here on earth *you* can't afford
the luxury.

In modern times, there has been only one Presidential
appointee who tried that sort of candor. He was Mike
DiSalle, the unknown mayor of Toledo appointed head of
the Office of Price Stabilization by President Truman.
Asked at his first press conference why the President had
chosen him, of all people, DiSalle patted his ample paunch
and said, "Maybe he wanted a man with *guts.*"

That single exchange destroyed DiSalle's future in
Washington. He finally retreated, defeated and in exile, to
become Governor of Ohio.

Unless you are willing to end up Governor of Ohio,
you must decide in all seriousness whether you became a
member of the cabinet because, to cite three common (and
mistaken) choices: (a) You are a close friend of the President; (b) You have a power base within the party; (c) You
are a genius.

In general, your choice should be based on your own
personality. Only you can really decide which of these
possibilities can be made plausible in terms of your own
history and character. You will be required continuously
to reinforce your image to three different constituencies:
the career civil servants in your department; your colleagues—i.e., rivals—in the cabinet; and the President himself, who will quickly forget why he really appointed you
and start judging you according to your own evaluation.

"You *can't* put that man in the cabinet, Mr. President,"

a White House aide once objected to Calvin Coolidge. "He's a perfect son-of-a-bitch!"

"Well," said Coolidge, "don't you think they have a right to be represented, too?"

If your secret hero is Genghis Khan, do not try to masquerade as St. Francis. There is room in Washington for everyone.

Before making your irrevocable decision, here are some of the questions you might want to consider in relation to the three possibilities mentioned above.

Do you really want to be a friend of the President?

Alpha and Omega, our end is contained in our beginning—and this option puts you in the same box with the President. He is unlikely to leave office with his reputation intact. This may be all right for *him*. He will retire with formal honors, if not gratitude, from his countrymen. He will be addressed for the rest of his life as Mr. President, while confidently awaiting the verdict of history. But what about you? The only cabinet officers history has ever deigned to acknowledge in any significant way were Washington's, Lincoln's, and the one who went to jail. Presumably you will still have a career to pursue, a life to live long after your President has faded into history. Do you really want to go down with him?

Helping a President make his mistakes out of loyalty is one thing; helping him for reasons of friendship is quite another. Reluctant loyalty can always be forgiven. A profitable book can even be written explaining the reluctance and justifying the loyalty. But friendship involves a commitment from which it might be hard to extricate yourself. Tradition will often condone misplaced loyalty; it is usually harsh on false friendships.

But the Omega aside, beginning your life in Washington as a friend of the President can be a serious handicap even in the Alpha stage. The President can probably be relied on not to deny the claim if it is advanced subtly (i.e., through a friendly newsman and not for attribution) and especially if it happens to be true. The danger is that by choosing to be the President's intimate you give the Washington press corps a handy criterion for measuring your performance from the very first day. How often do you have breakfast at the White House? How many weekends do you spend at Camp David? What is your mileage on Air Force One? No matter how satisfactorily these numbers may redound to your credit, that credit will be undermined every time the White House fails to support *in toto* the recommendations of the particular bureaucracy which you represent.

On the day this is written, for example, the *New York Times* offers an analysis of the first year of the Nixon administration, evaluating the performance of the cabinet. It contains the following paragraph:

The President's two other close associates [the first was Attorney General John Mitchell] among the 12 Cabinet members have turned out to be less formidable figures in Washington than some [i.e. the *New York Times*] at first presumed. William P. Rogers, the Secretary of State, and Robert H. Finch, the Secretary of Health, Education and Welfare, have not been inconspicuous, but their long friendship with Mr.

Nixon has not noticeably resulted in extradimensional bureaucratic power.

This happens to relate to a Republican administration, specifically Mr. Nixon's. But only a distaste for research prevents me from documenting similar first-year analyses from every other administration. The point is: why let yourself in for this sort of exposure? The odds are overwhelming. You will begin losing sooner, lose more at the end, and gain no particular advantage in between.

Arriving on the Washington scene as the President's friend also plunges you immediately into the game of Who Talked to the President Last? long before you can possibly be qualified to play it. This is the most rarefied, subtle game in the Capital. It is not for novices.

As played by cabinet officers, the game goes something like this:

Secretary A: "I just talked to the President and I'm afraid he's going to give me the action on that can of worms we discussed at the last cabinet meeting."

Secretary B: "That's odd. I just talked to the President myself. He gave me the distinct impression that *I* was going to have the action on that."

Secretary A: (*Pause*) "Uh . . . what time did *you* talk to him?"

The game of Who Talked to the President Last? as played by cabinet officers compares to the game as played by members of the White House staff approximately as checkers to chess, which will become apparent when we get to the subject of special assistants. Even within the cabinet, however, some are better positioned to play the game than others.

Secretary of the Interior Walter Hickel's celebrated letter suggesting that the President spend more time talking to his cabinet officers will probably endure as a classic example of a cabinet officer's first realization that he was losing a game, the existence of which he was previously unaware. As Presidential assistant Robert Haldeman subsequently indicated to reporters, it all depends on what you want to talk about. "The Postmaster General got in without any trouble all during the postal strike. Suppose Wally Hickel calls up at 2 A.M. and says there's been a disaster in oil pollution. He says, 'I've got to talk to the President.' He gets to talk to him."

(Most of this text was written before Secretary Hickel got into this game and I am truly sorry that, owing to my own indolence, it did not get into print in time to help him.)

Every cabinet member, of course, has a direct telephone line to the White House. He is theoretically free to use that line at any time. But can the Secretary of Transportation, for example, really call the President of the United States at midnight to say, "Mr. President, you will be happy to know that planes are now flying into JFK Airport in New York with an average delay of only two hours"? Can the Secretary of Housing and Urban Development call him to say, "Mr. President, I just wanted you to know that those seventeen building-trades unions in Chicago have finally agreed to negotiate with us through a single shop steward and Mayor Daley is now the only hold-out"?

Obviously not. Secretaries of State and Secretaries of Defense, however, make this kind of call to the President almost routinely. Consequently—and this is an axiom or, at least, a corollary—*Secretaries of Defense and Secretaries of State will always win the game of Who Talked to the President Last? unless they happen to be playing against each other or a member of the White House staff.*

Finally, basing your claim on "the President's trust and friendship" opens you to the charge of cronyism. It means that your political opposition (both in and out of your own party) can with a single word link you to Sherman Adams's coat, Harry Truman's deep freeze, and Warren Harding's sex life.

Who needs it?

Is it really safe to have your own power base within the party?

If there is any relationship more dangerous to a cabinet officer than being a friend of the President it is being the President's rival—no matter whether that rivalry is actual or potential. So long as it exists, or the President thinks it does, he will be nervous every time you walk into a cabinet meeting.

You will be expected from time to time to demonstrate your self-proclaimed prowess by delivering votes on the Hill. Every time the administration loses an important bill in the Congress, you may expect the President to look across that huge table in the cabinet room and demand an explanation. From you.

Presidents succeed because of their extraordinary qualities of leadership and their penetrating insights into the national needs; they fail only through lack of support from the Congress and their own subordinates. Think carefully before deciding how big a share in that failure you wish to apply for.

The greatest hazard you will encounter, should you decide to enter office as a power broker of your party, is that there is no party. Or, rather, that there are several dozen parties living in reluctant collaboration—on both sides of the political aisle—and no man can be a hero to more than one cabal of his nominal allies at the same time. Abraham Lincoln may be called as witness to this, as to so many other phenomena, proving that the condition has persisted a long time and also enabling me to avoid bringing in contemporary examples which might be misunderstood as partisanship.

Commenting on the political situation in 1848, Congressman Lincoln recalled the exclamation of an unfortunate constituent back in Illinois who was in process of being indicted for stealing hogs.

The clerk read on till he got to and through the words, "did steal, take, and carry away, ten boars, ten sows, ten shoats, and ten pigs," at which he exclaimed: "Well, by golly, that is the most equally divided gang of hogs I ever did hear of." If there is any other gang of hogs more equally divided than the Democrats of New York are about this time, I have not heard of it.

Of course, that was a long time ago. But the phenomenon is far from unknown today, and there are more states in the union.

Yet, you may say to yourself, there are always political currents within the national party—whatever that may be —so why can't I ride the stream which happens to be strongest at the moment?

I will tell you why.

To begin with, how do you imagine the President got where *he* is, which is occupying the biggest chair at the cabinet table? He has the odd notion that he represents the majority not only of his party but of the whole country. That's how he got elected. Unless you are prepared to demand that he move over—an unbelievably dangerous maneuver—you are left with the alternative of representing the *minority* faction of your party. In which case you will set in motion the following chain of unpleasant events.

Let's assume that your party is presently divided into two more or less recognizable factions. To avoid contemporary labels, we'll call them the *sea blues* and the *dinner greens*. (The scholarly reader may recognize these as two actual political factions of ancient Byzantium; I hope he will not consider them inappropriate for our illustration.) The dominant wing of your party, represented by the President, is the dinner greens. You are a hero of the sea blues, which represents perhaps forty percent of your party's strength in the Congress.

The scene is the family quarters at the White House (known variously as the "President's House," the "Mansion," or the "Residence" depending on the whim of the incumbent.) The time, about 1 A.M. The President and the First Lady are alone for the first time in sixteen hours.

First Lady: The cabinet meeting this morning: how did it go, dear?

The President: Great. One of the best we've had. I think the team is really getting into first gear. I've finally made them understand that the country only has one President at a time and that in this administration it happens to be me. Whether they like it or not.

First Lady: Why *shouldn't* they like it, dear? After all, the Constitution says the whole Executive Branch is just an extension of the Presidency. Besides, they owe everything to you. Nobody ever heard of any of them until you put them into the cabinet.

The President: The only one of the whole bunch who's ever *read* the Constitution is the Attorney General. And *he* only reads it because he enjoys telling me that my whole program is unconstitutional. I can handle the A.G. But that bastard Truehardt is getting to be a real pain.

First Lady: But, dear, I thought getting him into the administration was one of your real coups. Everyone says so. After all, he represents the sea blue wing of the party. Isn't he why we can all stand united against the opposition?

The President: You've been talking to Truehardt's wife.

First Lady: Shouldn't I? I thought I was supposed to be gracious to *all* the cabinet wives.

The President: Of course you are, darling. But be

damned careful about what you say around the Truehardts. He'd like nothing better than to see me fall flat on my face. The sea blues lost in the primaries, they lost in the convention, and they'll never forgive me for beating them. Sometimes I feel safer dealing with the opposition. There are plenty of spiritual dinner greens over there, anyhow. A hell of a lot more than in that bunch around Truehardt.

First Lady: Well, dear, if you feel that strongly why don't you just ask him to resign?

The President: Are you kidding? With the administration only six months old? It would wreck the party.

First Lady: Then what are you going to do?

The President: I'll tell you what I'm going to do. I'm going to take H.R. 13202 and H.R. 13506 and S. 907 and give Mr. Truehardt the job of getting them passed on the floor—every damned one of them.

First Lady: I don't know what those are.

The President: Never mind what they are. I'm not going to stay up all night discussing politics. You know how I hate politics. But I will say this: those are two House bills and one Senate bill the sea blues just can't *stand*. We'll let their hero, Secretary Truehardt, go up there and try to change their minds. Either we'll get the legislation, which I doubt, or our sea blue friends will start looking for a new hero. Either way, I win.

First Lady: But suppose Mr. Truehardt won't support those bills? After all, he's a sea blue himself, isn't he?

The President: Don't be naïve, darling. He took the cabinet job, didn't he?

Princes of the realm have never taken kindly to barons who vie with them for power. King John may have knuckled under at Runnymede. But, though many have tried, no Magna Carta has ever been forced upon an American President by members of his own cabinet. Remembering this will make your cabinet career both longer and more tranquil.

Do you have the makings of a genius—and is it wise?

Practically speaking, the only cabinet members who can hope to succeed as geniuses are the Secretary of the Treasury and the Secretary of Defense. No one else is surrounded by the requisite staff of experts in arcane fields and, more important, habitually makes his public utterances in an exceedingly complex technical jargon, usually associated with the Harvard Business School, but which can in fact be traced back to the Delphic oracle and the Gordian knot.

Yet genius does come easier to any cabinet officer than to ordinary men or women. For one thing you are the beneficiary of that aura which even cynical citizens project around the head anointed by high office. A distinguished attorney from Tennessee who participated for several months in the Army-McCarthy hearings of the early 1950's was asked years later what had been his principal experience in Washington.

It was disillusionment. "I had always thought," he said, "that people who get elected to the Senate or appointed to the cabinet must have something a little special about them. It was kind of sad and depressing to discover that they're no different from the guys who hang around the courthouse here in Memphis."

Part of your strength lies in the fact that relatively few citizens perceive this. You will be expected during your tenure in office to avoid disillusioning them.

The technique of being a cabinet genius is relatively simple. After all, you have the resources of the whole federal government at your command, as well as your own department of thousands or even hundreds of thousands, many of whom are quite intelligent. All you need is a good memory and a willingness to do homework. Nor will your homework be nearly so onerous as the burden inflicted upon your school-age children trying to master something truly difficult, like the new math.

Remember, if you call the meeting, you will generally control the subject of that meeting. If you are able and willing to spend a few hours the night before memorizing some obscure facts about specialized subjects, you will enter the conference with more than enough ammunition to intimidate all but the most foolhardy—and precious few of those ever become prominent enough to attend cabinet-level meetings.

As a resident genius, you will want to follow one important rule: *Never take an assistant to meetings.* This alone will make you conspicuous. Every other principal will bring at least one technical expert, if not an entire staff. He will do this even if he was, say, the world's leading nuclear physicist before assuming his present position and knows far more about the subject under discussion than anyone else in his department. He is merely being true to the Washington Way, best expressed in the maxim that "nobody ever writes anything he signs, and no one signs anything he writes."

If you, however, come alone armed with a headful of highly selective data, you start with an enormous moral advantage. At a moment of your own choosing, you will say something like this: "What bothers me is the long-range effect of all this on the coal industry. It's all very well to talk about domestic fuel oil, but if you look at the probable effect of reducing the quotas on imported residual fuel oil as a function of price, you can see that by the middle 1970's 38 cents per 1,000 btu's will not even be competitive with nuclear power, let alone oil. It's obvious what that will mean to the coal industry."

Few things have been less obvious since Kant's *Critique of Pure Reason*, but no one at the meeting will say so. Rather, the Secretary of the Interior (if he is your target) will have to huddle with his fuel-oil specialist, who in turn will need a moment to consult his statistical tables. Or, better still, he may ask you to clarify the question. You can say anything you like in the way of clarification; as long as you say it with authority nobody will display his ignorance twice by admitting that the second statement makes even less sense than the first.

The important thing is to sit quietly, not quite concealing your impatience, while the other participants acquaint themselves with the basic facts, which, obviously, they should have learned before coming to this meeting and wasting your valuable time.

You will be assisted in your game by a venerable Washington custom. Caste is rather strictly observed, as one should expect in the capital city of the world's leading democracy, with the result that only principals—that is, the senior officials present—are permitted to sit at the center table. Everybody else sits in chairs along the wall. If the room is a large one, it may be necessary for your conferees to summon their technical experts from the far shadows to whisper their advice. Your patient silence as you watch these migrations will be eloquent.

Before adopting this stance, however, you would do well to consider that the ordinary mortal, as Schopenhauer observed long ago, "looks upon the genius much as we look upon a hare, which is good to eat after it has been killed and dressed up. So long as it is alive, it is only good to shoot at." On the other hand, since you will be shot at anyhow, the risk may be worthwhile. At least you will be popular with the President. You will be an ornament to his administration without posing a threat of possible future competition. As a successful politician, he will be quite confident that no man with a public reputation for "genius" will ever be supported by the American people for the nation's highest office. This is part of the collective wisdom that kept Alexander Hamilton out of the White House and which may yet see us to our two hundredth anniversary.

Lincoln, who had a terrible time with cabinet officers, once remarked of his Secretary of War, "We may have to treat Stanton as they are sometimes obliged to treat a Methodist minister I know out West. He gets wrought up to so high a pitch of excitement in his prayers and exhortations that they put bricks in his pockets to keep him down. But I guess we'll let him jump awhile first."

Sooner or later, the President will put rocks in your pockets. There are no successful cabinet officers. So long as our national problems remain impervious to short-term solutions, failure will be part of every cabinet secretary's job description. Better you than the President. But, in the face of this destiny, there are still alternatives.

In the Mosaic ritual of the Day of Atonement, two goats were chosen, not one, as is commonly believed. The first goat was sacrificed. The other was sent alive into the wilderness, the sins of the people having been symbolically laid upon it. It is that latter unfortunate beast we know as the scapegoat. But at least he had a chance.

If you must be a goat, a scapegoat is not necessarily the worst kind of goat to be.

Whatever path you ultimately choose—which, as previously stated, should be something you can sustain throughout what might, to everyone's surprise, turn out to be a long Washington career—try to adhere to one basic philosophy of cabinet officering which should underly all your actions. This can best be illustrated by an anecdote.

Some years ago I was with a small group being flown ashore from the aircraft carrier *Roosevelt*, a hundred miles out in the Atlantic. We were issued bright orange life jackets and strapped into our seats, facing backward, by a cheerful young naval officer. He directed our attention to two straps hanging down from either side of the jackets. In the absolutely unlikely event of this perfectly routine flight encountering some unusual difficulty—such as falling into the ocean—we should consider pulling one of the straps, but not both.

"This one releases a shark repellent," he said. "And this one releases a dye that will make it easier to locate you from the air. But don't use both at the same time because they neutralize each other."

So it is in the cabinet. *You must decide whether you want to repel sharks or to attract attention. You cannot do both.*

3

The Open Mouth

Stranger, pass gently over this sod. If he opens his mouth,
you're gone, by God!   —EPITAPH TO A WESTERN POLITICIAN

NOW THAT NUDITY has taken over the stage,
politics is the sole remaining branch of show business where
importance is still attached to the spoken word. Until
women in politics become more frequent and the men
handsomer, this situation is likely to persist.

On the other hand, little of what is said is spontaneous.
The average statesman comes to the podium with a prepared text—and often, too, a handful of 3-by-5 file cards
labeled "ad libs." Somebody has to write all this. If you are
among those who suffer from the fairly common belief
that you possess something known as "literary talent," you
will doubtless view this as an opportunity.

It is not an opportunity. Quite the opposite. I do not
expect you to believe this because, as has been pointed out
in another connection, there are some things which cannot
be made clear to a virgin by either words or pictures.

A few weeks after I arrived in Washington to write
speeches for the Secretary of Defense (or to become, in
the words of an erudite friend, "a flamen to Mars"), I was
taken to lunch at the Federal City Club. My host was an

old friend, Abram Chayes, then the Legal Advisor at the State Department. At a nearby table sat Arthur Schlesinger, Jr., who had recently left the White House to devote full time to his book on JFK. Believing myself to be the only man in Washington who had never met Mr. Schlesinger, I solicited an introduction, which my friend Mr. Chayes chose to make in the following manner.

"My friend here," he said, "wonders whether writing speeches for other men to deliver can be considered a respectable form of human endeavor."

"No," said Mr. Schlesinger.

I did not believe him then and you will not believe me now. The best I can hope to do for you is to repeat Lord Chesterfield's advice to his son: Since you must dance, learn how to do it well so as not to appear ridiculous although engaged in an absurd occupation.

Know What to Expect

YOU WILL GO into your Washington assignment with heady visions of yourself during the late hours of the night, at the right hand of the President or a cabinet secretary, nudging History onto a new track with a brilliant epigram, or a profound metaphor, or possibly even a New Idea. At last, you have the ear of the mighty.

So does the great man's barber.

But since there is no dissuading a literary man from charging through the gates of power once he imagines them to have been opened to him, I will confine myself to a few

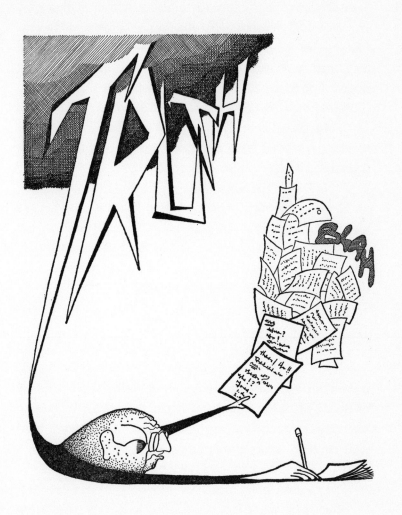

words of advice about how to make yourself marginally useful.

Unlike bright young men from the Harvard Law School, or even the University of Chicago School of Business, the average writer's idea of power is a parking permit in the State Department basement, the River Entrance to the Pentagon, or—is it possible?—White House limousine service. No matter how rich or successful—Robert Sherwood, for example was a rich and famous playwright when *he* went to the White House—the professional writer is essentially a man who makes his living picking up coal along the railroad tracks. When he finds himself suddenly wrenched from his accustomed rounds and brought to stand before kings, the results are painfully predictable.

As a writer you will have developed a touching faith in the power of words. You believe, with Mark Twain, that "the difference between the right word and the almost right word is the difference between lightning and the lightning bug." You are not here to make policy (that ambition will come later). All you want to do is *communicate.* And, while you are struggling to choose between the lightning and the lightning bug, somebody who could not unassisted compose a ten-word telegram will walk away with the game.

The name of the game is Who Controls the Final Draft?

Having lost this game at least as often as I won it, I will cite the more authoritative testimony of Mr. Dean

Acheson, whose memoirs offer a classic example of the game as played by a Grand Master.

During his early days as an Assistant Secretary of State, Mr. Acheson tells us, he was periodically summoned, together with his peers, to help Secretary Cordell Hull review the final draft of his forthcoming speech, which had invariably been drafted by Mr. Hull's principal speech writer, one Leo Pasvolsky. Writes Mr. Acheson:

> I submitted to this routine, if not docilely, at least with resignation, until this fateful day in April 1944 when, on receiving the usual slip, I threw it in the wastebasket and went on with the problems presented by the European neutrals. The next morning the same thing happened. Then the Secretary's messenger summoned me to the presence. Mr. Hull looked pained.
> "Are you refusing to come to my speech meeting?" he asked. I explained that I was and why it was a waste of time to go through the form of editing Leo's liturgy. He seemed surprised and with hardly more than a trace of sarcasm said: "I suppose you think that you could write a better speech." I said one could certainly try.
> He suggested that I do so and gave me the existing draft. I had long waited for an opportunity . . .

This shows you what the Leos of Washington are up against. *You cannot win this game by improving your prose style.*

Successful Washington speech writing is one percent literary talent and ninety-nine percent political in-fighting. The first rule in that combat is: *Never, never do today what you can put off until tomorrow.*

The halls may be filled with ambitious young men waiting to improve on your product, in the process somehow transforming it into *their* product. But, you may depend on it, nobody will stay up all night writing a competing draft. Or, if one does, there is always the chance that it will be given to you to edit.

For the corollary of the first rule of political speech writing is: *The number of times a speech must be rewritten is directly proportional to the time remaining before it must be delivered.*

In other words, if you climb aboard the plane with a "final" draft and the flight time to your destination is three and one-half hours, you will be required to rewrite the speech four times—assuming one hour to be the normal minimum time required for a full rewrite. If you are not aboard the aircraft, someone else will do these rewrites— and by the time the plane returns, your job will be hanging by an extremely thin thread.

The best defense against this is never to let your brain child out of your sight until that magical moment when it emerges, like Minerva, full-blown from the head of Zeus. At the instant of delivery, it becomes the Boss's speech and thus immune to criticism by your colleagues (who can never be sure how much of it was *you* and how much *him*.)

Retaining control of your offspring until it reaches the portals of birth requires great skill. Also luck, and manifestations of character which will not be a source of pride for your grandchildren. Yet it is essential.

There are some situations, of course, in which it is impossible. During my own years in the White House, I observed that no speech draft—be it the most innocuous after-

dinner toast or the mildest of airport greetings—ever came
from the State Department with less than seven sets of
initials indicating approval and helpful editing. Of course,
not even the Lord's Prayer could survive that much help
and I was occasionally tempted to telephone the owner of
the bottom set of initials to ask whether he might not have
the original draft of his suggested remarks, which could be
counted upon to be superior to the version that had
finally emerged at the top of the escalator. But, I invariably
reflected, the unfortunate author of the original was doubtless a young man ambitiously pursuing a career that could
be irreparably ruined by a telephone conversation with
the White House over the heads of six senior officers. So
we ignored the output of the State Department and did
the best we could.

If fate has situated you close to the seat of power,
however, opportunities will occasionally arise which will
almost compensate for the frustrations of what is essentially
an improper occupation for a grown man. Mr. Acheson
himself has said, "I have long been the advocate of the
heretical view that, whatever political scientists might say,
policy in this country is made, as often as not, by the neces-
sity of finding something to say for an important figure com-
mitted to speak without a prearranged subject." Charles
Schultze, then Director of the Bureau of the Budget, once
complained to me that "the real menace to a balanced
budget around here isn't the departments: it's the speech
writers." This was shortly after my colleague Robert
Hardesty and I had solved a speech-writing problem at two

o'clock in the morning by creating a new "program" with a sexy title which could be used in a Presidential bill-signing ceremony the following morning in the East Room. The last time I looked at that "program" it carried a price tag of $140,000,000. It was and is a good program for which I make no apologies and which I will not undermine by revealing. But how many chances does a writer get to commit that kind of money to a worthy cause with three paragraphs on a single sheet of paper?

Perhaps the greatest compensation for the Washington writer is instant publication. In real life weeks, months, and, not infrequently, years may elapse between conception and the birth of a wise thought or a well-turned phrase. As an assistant to a major political figure, you may sometimes achieve "publication" within minutes and read the "reviews" within hours. The happiest occasions are those where public duties and private inclinations come serendipitously together. Here is an example.

On April 27, 1966, the Prime Minister of Denmark, Jens Otto Krag, was entertained at a state dinner in the White House. This called, of course, for a formal toast by the President of the United States—the draft of which I completed about 1 A.M. of the same day. This was, the perceptive reader will have noted, a violation of my own rule about premature completion of speech drafts, but this was an exceptional occasion.

It happens that there is a lady in Denmark whose friendship I (and my wife) have cherished for many years. She is a much-traveled person with whom we had somehow lost touch. It also happens that when I visited Denmark in the late 1940's, the lady's father had presented me with a small book containing his reflections on the causes of the Second World War. Now, the lady's father was a distinguished maritime lawyer, but this was his only venture into general prose and it attracted little attention then or later. Until the 28th of April, 1966, that is.

On the previous evening, the President of the United States offered the Prime Minister of Denmark what I confess to believing to be one of the more felicitous toasts recently afforded a visiting statesman.

"Mr. Prime Minister:

"One of my countrymen has said that although he never really expects to see Heaven, it is all right—because he has seen Denmark.

"Mr. Prime Minister, I have not seen Heaven either. But I, too, have seen Denmark. So I know what to look forward to.

"Or, at least, what to hope for.

"We have a saying in this country that good things usually come in small packages. This is not easy for a native of Texas to admit. But when we look at your own country, it just can't be denied.

"What most of the human race still seeks and prays for in the future is already part of Denmark's history.

"In so many ways, you in Denmark have been a shining example for the rest of the world to follow. We in America are proud of our free public schools. But Denmark's public schools were a reality while ours were still only a noble ideal.

"We are proud of our recent achievements in caring for our sick and providing for our aged. Yet, we are really only acquiring today what you have had for nearly a century.

"We are today engaged in a great national effort to improve our American cities. We want to make all of them places of health and beauty, as well as convenience. And when the doubters and the critics tell me that it can't be done, I say to them: Go look at Copenhagen.

"Above all, your countrymen—the descendants of the Viking warriors—are now leaders in the world's desperate search for lasting peace.

"One of your Danish authors has rightly written:

"'Look at us, follow our example; learn from our peaceful civilization. . . . See how we, who not so many centuries ago were at war with each other, have reached the point where we consider war an absolutely ridiculous and antiquated method of settling disputes. But as a rule no citizens of the great nations . . . listen to these shouts because practically speaking nobody there understands our language.'

"Mr. Prime Minister, let me assure you that we Americans do understand your language. For it is also ours. It is the language of peace. And it calls for a world where men can say of every nation what they now say of yours—

> "'And her ways are ways of pleasantness,
> And all her paths are peace.'

"Ladies and gentlemen, I give you King Frederik and Queen Ingrid."

I remarked to my wife after dinner that now, by God, we would hear from Birte. And we did. The quotation appeared on the front page of every paper in Copenhagen and a few days later I received a letter addressed to me at the White House—that particular quotation having only one possible sponsor on the North American continent.

This is doubtless a splendid example of how touchingly simple is a writer's notion of power and influence, like parking space at the Pentagon. The episode does contain, however, at least two examples of survival technique for the political speech writer—despite its violation of the last-minute rule.

First, the remarks contain what might be called technical information, i.e., something so obscure that it can be explained only by the true author. In this case, it was the source of the quotation. When the Danish embassy and the wire services began calling the White House to identify the Danish writer so suddenly elevated to international celebrity, there was only one man on the staff who could answer the question—which is as close to a copyright as the ghost writer can ever hope to get.

The moral goes something like this: deal with your principal directly whenever possible (hence the last-minute rule); when this is not possible—as often it will not be—include in the original draft something likely to survive the rewrites, the key to which is known only to you. Like all moves in a game of Monopoly played for real money, this will not be easy. You will be asked to name the father by every social worker into whose loving care your orphan speech chances to fall. (They will *hesitate* to ask because this necessitates admitting that they do not know, an admission which the Greeks considered the beginning of wisdom, but one which does not immediately leap to the tongues of those with whom you will be dealing.)

Your response to all such requests from intermediaries, therefore, should be: "You mean *you* don't know? That surprises me. Actually, I don't know either—I got it from the Boss. I thought *he* must have gotten it from *you.*"

This will end the questions until the speech is finally presented to the Boss and he says, "Where the hell did you get *this?*" At that point they will have to send for you, and the true authorship of the document will be apparent.

I have assumed in the foregoing that you have sufficient access to the Boss—be he President, cabinet officer or whomever—to make this ploy work. If you do have such access, the corollary is: *Remember, nobody but you and the Boss knows what was said while you were alone together in the elevator.*

If you do not have that kind of access you should stop writing speeches and get out of the government.

The second lesson to be derived from the Danish episode is that, for a writer, ceremonial occasions are likely to provide more professional satisfactions and fewer slashes of the sword from one's fellow courtiers than such major occasions as the State of the Union Message. Ceremonies involve more style than substance. Even the lawyers know this, which is the only reason they tolerate speech writers. They will leave you alone on the small, insignificant occasions in which much can be accomplished—if only you do not attract undue attention.

A good press notice is for a speech writer, especially a White House speech writer, what a reputation for "independence" is for a politician—it attracts lightning. In speech writing, as elsewhere, the best art is that which conceals itself.

In recent years, to be sure, there has been a tendency on the part of some ghost writers to make themselves highly visible. This will be a shortlived phenomenon and Washington speech writers will return to decent anonymity, if only because it is becoming increasingly apparent that public figures tend to be just as bright before meeting their favorite speech writer as afterward, and that the writer's brilliance has a way of dimming as soon as his particular star exits the political stage.

The hardest thing for a writer to remember is that original truth is not discovered by rearranging words. A speech writer is engaged in an essentially Jesuitical operation: his business is to find arguments for the truth which has been revealed elsewhere, usually a few feet down the hall.

If this sounds cynical, perhaps you should stay out of the speech-writing business—and politics.

A venerable but still popular Washington anecdote, often attributed to the late Senator Everett Dirksen, concerns a young schoolteacher appearing before the school board of a rural Southern community.

"Before we hire you, young man," one of the elders demanded, "I want a direct answer to this question: do you believe the world was created in six days, like it says in the Bible; or do you believe in the theory of evolution?"

The young man reflected.

"I can teach it either way," he said.

A political speech writer is engaged in what Professor Schopenhauer called "the art of controversial dialectic." It is a necessary art, if an impure one, because a man may be objectively in the right and still come off worst in the eyes of his audience—or even his own.

"If the reader asks how this is," says the good doctor, "I reply that it is simply the natural baseness of human nature. If human nature were not base, but thoroughly honorable, we should in every debate have no other aim than the discovery of truth; we should not in the least care whether the truth proved to be in favor of the opinion which we had begun by expressing, or of the opinion of our adversary."

If men were angels, said Alexander Hamilton, government would be unnecessary.

Schopenhauer really ought to be canonized as the patron saint of speech writers. He not only understood the craft, but found reasons to legitimatize it—which few have succeeded in doing since.

"This very dishonesty," he tell us, "this persistence in a proposition which seems false even to ourselves, has something to be said for it. It often happens that we begin with the firm conviction of the truth of our statement, but our opponent's argument appears to refute it. Should we abandon our position at once, we may discover later on that we were right after all. The proof we offered was false, but nevertheless there was a proof for our statement which was true. The argument which would have been our salvation did not occur to us at the moment. Hence we make it a rule to attack a counter-argument, even though to all appearances it is true and forcible, in the belief that its truth is only superficial, and that in the course of the dispute another argument will occur to us by which we may upset it, or succeed in confirming the truth of our statement."

Ours is an age when dead philosophers are rarely consulted as guides to contemporary decisions. If you can read, as well as write, you will find this a significant advantage.

It was, for example, Professor Schopenhauer who really put Barry Goldwater's finger on the nuclear trigger in the 1964 American Presidential campaign.

Specifically, Strategy XXVIII, or the *Argumentum ad auditores.* Look it up.

As applied to the '64 campaign, the principle was brought to bear in response to a particularly unfortunate (from the Senator's view) speech to the annual convention of the Veterans of Foreign Wars in Detroit. Senator Goldwater was concerned with what he conceived to be an irrational phobia against tactical nuclear weapons. His argument was that, using tactical nuclear weapons, it is now possible to produce artillery barrages on the battlefield no different in magnitude of violence from the heavy artillery of past wars. We are the only nation which has an arsenal of such weapons and it is foolish to tie our hands behind our back, argued Senator Goldwater, because of a self-imposed taboo. He called for the creation of a new category, to be known as "conventional nuclear weapons."

It fell to me to draft the first response to that speech from the incumbent administration, delivered two days later to the same audience. There is, of course, a very definite reason why this country has refrained from the use of tactical nuclear weapons. It has to do with *limited options*, *trip wires*, and *points-of-no-return*, not to mention minor nuisances such as nuclear fallout. All of which add up to the reaffirmation of an ancient philosophical conundrum about how a difference in degree becomes imperceptibly a difference in kind. In short, we do not use tactical nuclear weapons because, once the door is opened, there will be precious little time to debate the difference between "tactical" and "strategic." How small is "little?" How large is "big?" And, in a war, how concerned will the loser be with definitions?

There may be someone with enough talent to present that kind of argument to the VFW after they have been convening for a week in Detroit, but it's not me. Instead, I recalled the Professor's rule, and reflected on the fact that almost nobody understands the difference between a modal average and a simple arithmetic average, and acted accordingly.

Being in a unique position to do so, I ascertained the

number of tactical nuclear warheads then in our arsenal, and also the total megatonnage of that arsenal. Dividing one into the other, it was possible to construct such sentences as "How *conventional* was the bomb dropped on Hiroshima? The *average* explosive power of the weapons in our tactical nuclear arsenal is many times that of the Hiroshima bomb."

Technically correct. And enough to give pause for thought, even to a VFW convention in Detroit on a hot summer's night. Senator Goldwater's people struggled with that speech—and what grew out of it—for the rest of the campaign. I was, near the end, sorry for them. Every time they tried to refute the argument, they succeeded only in curling their candidate's finger tighter around that nuclear trigger.

The turnover rate for Washington speech writers is rather higher than for professional ball players. Some wangle promotions into "policy-making" jobs, some (a small minority) part company with their principal over matters of conscience, some are fired for incompetence (usually resulting from intemperance), and still more simply develop an incurable case of pitcher's elbow from too many trips to the mound. Chances are that, having ignored the advice offered at the beginning of this chapter to stay out of the ghost-writing business in the first place, you will one day wish to resign. Winston Churchill used to say that knowing *how* to resign is an essential part of the art of government. And here the imaginative speech writer has a unique opportunity.

There is a Washington story about a legendary writer who rose with his principal through the ranks, from the city council to the state legislature to the Congress to the United States Senate. Along the route, he became increasingly aware that he shared a problem with some of the boss's occasional lady friends: deeply appreciated the night before, but an irritating presence the morning after. You will find that this is not an uncommon phenomenon. If last night's speech was a bomb, you are this morning living proof of who caused the debacle; if last night was a rhetorical triumph, you are an irritating reminder to the boss that he is not necessarily another Daniel Webster.

Anyhow, our hero decided to resign. Such was his relationship to the Senator that for many years the Senator had rarely bothered to examine drafts of his speeches before the time came to present them. On this occasion, the solon mounted confidently to the podium and launched into the first page of his prepared text. It read something like this:

"There are those who say we cannot control inflation and still have full employment. I say we can—and I am going to tell you how.

"There are those who say we cannot contain Communist expansion and still have peace. I say we can—and I'm going to tell you how.

"There are those who say we cannot control riots in the streets and student demonstrations without political repression. I say we can—and I'm going to tell you how."

Whereupon the Senator turned the page and found, in the familiar handwriting of his loyal ghost, the following: "O.K., *you son-of-a-bitch, you're on your own. I have resigned.*"

4

What Do Special Assistants Specialize In?

His title seems to be Special Assistant to the President, or maybe Consultant. But don't be impressed. . . . Everybody in the place, and it is a big place, seemed to be a Special Assistant to the President except the towel man.　　　—MILTON MAYER IN *The Progressive*

NO ONE KNOWS EXACTLY when government assistants first became "special," and there is reason to believe that the title has begun to depreciate. Special assistants may be semantic descendants of the "special prosecutors" and "special investigators" of the 1920's and '30's, appointed to help local police departments find the still or horse parlor someone had secretly installed in the courthouse basement.

Until recently, the title was used mainly to describe a political appointee slipped into the organization chart somewhere between the Boss and the career civil service. Early in President Nixon's administration, however, the White House let it be known that plain "Assistant to the President" would henceforth be the senior title.

During President Johnson's administration, the Chief Clerk of the White House became Exeutive Assistant to the President and people who used to be "secretaries" to members of Congress have long since become "administrative assistants," no doubt to distinguish them from the lady "stenographers" who insisted on being called "secretaries."

So there are assistants, staff assistants, special assistants, special consultants, and various other brands of supernumeraries. (For some months, I dealt frequently with one unfortunate gentleman whose true and legal title was Special Assistant to the President of the United States for the Peaceful Reconstruction of Vietnam.) But for the moment, at least, "special" assistant retains a certain aura which makes it the most useful title for purposes of introduction to the genre.

Let us assume, therefore, that you are about to become a special assistant to a cabinet officer. Your existence will soon be a daily affront to a good many people. But your title, whether you wear it humbly or with average arrogance, will be a source of reassurance to the same people that you are a temporary phenomenon. Unless you are an especially virulent specimen, you can probably be tolerated until your "principal" (Washington's euphemism for "boss") loses the bureaucratic fight and resigns or gets fired.

To you, the adjective "special" is a mark of distinction attesting to your close relationship with the Chief (another euphemism) and marking you as a member of the oleiferous elite which floats upon the dull waters of the career civil service. To those looking up from the depths, that same badge is assurance that the tide will eventually float you away.

By whatever title you are known, you will be expected, if not exactly to waste your fragrance on the desert air, at least to bloom unseen. This, of course, you will not do—assuming that you have any real aptitude for the profession into which you are about to enter. You have been briefly touched by the finger of power; your business is to convert this opportunity into the more negotiable commodity of personal fame. This, after the captains and the kings depart, just may be translatable into real wealth.

There are rules to this game, as to any other, and you have precious little time in which to learn them. You must absorb them during the brief period while you are still educable. That is, while you are not yet or only very recently a special assistant and can therefore accept the notion that there is still something you do not know.

Rule Number One is: *The true special assistant is a specialist in nothing.* Please read that again. It does not mean what you think it does. Being a specialist in nothing is not really the same as knowing nothing, or having no usable skill. There are millions carrying impeccable credentials for the latter conditions of whom the world will never hear. *Specializing* in nothing, if done properly, can lead on to fame and fortune. But it requires technique.

The specialist in nothing is popularly known as a "generalist"—a word which has come to describe those in any profession who have risen above the intellectual limitations of their craft. The man who fails to so rise will be viewed by his superiors as a piece of dough which is all lump and no leaven, useful when kneaded but not something to be served at state banquets. Great engineers get to be presidents of automobile companies only after proving that they are no longer mere engineers; physicists get to be chairmen of physics departments by becoming more than mere scientists; economists achieve executive status by learning to speak English. Lawyers—and if you are a Washington special assistant the odds are overwhelming that this is your profession—must overcome the handicap laid on them by Professor Morris Cohen's observation that "the law sharpens the mind by narrowing it."

You can accomplish this most effectively by turning your colleague's own professional expertise against him. Practice lines like: "That's an exceedingly well-developed proposal, George, but I'm afraid the Secretary won't buy it. He wants more than just a *legal* solution," and "That's procedurally very ingenious, Larry. But I'm afraid the Secretary is going to want much more substantive content on this one."

Variations for the other professions are obvious. If you are an economist among economists, you might say, "The Secretary is not interested in models on this one, fellows. He wants a pragmatic, on-line proposal."

For the scientist, of whatever discipline, the standard, all-purpose conference opener is: "Gentlemen, I have assured the Secretary that we will *try* not to be parochial about this."

Note that there is a common thread running through all these remarks. Each makes clear that, as special assistant, *you* are the authority on what the Secretary thinks. This

is your real field of specialization. You must convince the
entire staff of the truth of that proposition—without, however, letting the Secretary himself get wind of what you
are up to. "Ambition often puts men upon doing the
meanest offices," said Jonathan Swift, "so climbing is performed in the same posture as creeping."

In the Secretary's mind, you are basically a high-
priced male secretary. He views you as a convenience and
an expediter—someone through whom he can issue instructions to a dozen people at once: "Tell Smith I want a
report on that California situation by Friday. . . . Tell
Jones I need a rundown on the appropriations bill not later
than noon Friday. . . . Tell Doakes I'd like to know what
the hell is holding up the nonfunctional buttonhole
study . . ." and so forth.

It does not really require a *magna cum laude* graduate
of the Harvard Law School to perform this function, but
your education should enable you to take advantage of the
situation in which you fortuitously find yourself. Everything
depends on how you relay the Secretary's instructions.

You can, for example write a memorandum like the
following:

TO: Assistant Secretary for Uniform Standards
FROM: The Special Assistant
SUBJECT: Naval Uniforms

The Secretary is extremely concerned about what, if anything,
the Navy intends to do about the nonfunctional buttonholes
in the uniforms of enlisted seamen. He would appreciate a
report on this matter by the close of business Friday.

You can write such a memo, that is, if you intend to remain an obscure and powerless junior member of the establishment for the remainder of your career. If you intend to get anyplace, your memorandum will read:

TO: Assistant Secretary for Uniform Standards
FROM: The Special Assistant
SUBJECT: Naval Uniforms

The Secretary has asked me to look into the Navy's interminable delay in deciding what to do about the nonfunctional buttonholes in sailors' uniforms. I see no reason to hold a meeting about this. But it would be appreciated if a status report on this problem could be submitted to my office not later than the close of business on Thursday.

By these methods you will soon have everybody in the department, including those who theoretically outrank you, reporting to the Secretary through *you*. Initially, some unusually stalwart appointee who appears in the organization table immediately below the Secretary's box, who has been confirmed by the Congress, and who is twice your age may object to "taking orders from kids" and complain. Your defense is simple. You confess failure.

"I've been expecting that, Mr. Secretary. Apparently Smith and I have the wrong chemistry. He just plain doesn't like me. He's been making it abundantly clear that unless he gets his instructions directly from you he's going to ignore them."

This will elicit from the Secretary the observation that there is no room in the government for prima donnas, and certainly not in *his* department. He will then make clear to Smith that he is no better than any of the other

Assistant Secretaries and that—damn it—we're all here to do a job, not to waste our time on protocol and injured feelings.

So much for Assistant Secretary Smith. But be careful. You may be unlucky enough to encounter an operator who knows how to fight back. He does this by ignoring you. He doesn't return your phone calls. He doesn't respond to your memos—and if asked about one, at lunch perhaps, blandly denies having seen it. Or your memos may come back to you with a little rubber-stamped line at the bottom which says, "Asst. Secretary Jones Has Seen," a grace note placed there by his secretary and translatable as "Mr. Jones looked at this and said you should go ⸻ yourself."

If this should happen, you, in turn, must ignore Jones. Do not try to fight. Jones is a pro and, at this stage in your career, out of your class.

The first rule of memo writing is: *Make everybody report back to you, and by a specific deadline—preferably one designed to make somebody work all night.* The corollary to this rule is: *There is nothing you can do about anyone who has the balls to throw your memos into the wastebasket.* (Note example of this technique as applied by former Secretary of State Dean Acheson, page 54).

It is important to remember this, but don't let it worry you: the odds against encountering any such person in the federal bureaucracy are on the order of ten thousand to one, odds which the theory of probability tells us we can safely ignore. But do keep it in mind, if only to avoid the embarrassment of the celebrated statistician who drowned while fording a river with a mean average depth of 3½ feet. Remember, in the higher echelons of government, people who think they can afford to ignore you usually can.

Climbing the Pyramids

THE PURPOSE OF POWER, as every special assistant knows, is the acquisition of more power. To use effectively the leverage inherent in your position you need a clear insight into the true distribution of power in government hierarchies. The easiest way is to view the government and each department within it as a series of pyramids built upon pyramids. Let us take, as our example, the Department of Defense.

Within DOD (as it is usually known to its friends) we find the Department of the Army, the Department of the Air Force, and the Navy Department. Within the Navy Department (for reasons I was never able to discover, the Navy dislikes the word "of") we also find the Marine Corps, which is a formidable pyramid in its own right.

Now, each of these departments is its own little pyramid—the technical definition of which is "a solid whose base surface is a straight-sided figure and whose side surfaces are triangles having the side lines of the base as their base lines and their vertices meeting in one point called the apex or summit." This, in case the thought never occurred to you, is why the most glamorous of international meet-

ings are called "summit" meetings. It also explains the nature of your power as a special assistant. Within, say, the Department of the Army, an officer in the field may have to walk the entire base of the pyramid to communicate with the appropriate officer of another branch of the service. Indeed, regulations may *forbid* him to make that journey; he may be required to launch his thoughts vertically toward the apex of the pyramid, wait for them to be sent back down again toward the other side of the pyramid's base, returned to the apex and, finally, back down to himself. But the apex of this particular pyramid is the Secretary of the Army. What may be for a famous, much-honored major general the equivalent of a trip around the world is for the Secretary's special assistant merely a stroll across the hall. This is the true source of your power.

Resting upon these pyramids, however, is another pyramid known as the Office of the Secretary of Defense. At the base of *this* pyramid are the various Assistant Secretaries —the Assistant Secretary for Manpower, the Assistant Secretary for Installations and Logistics, the Assistant Secretary for Administration, etc. They are spread out along the E ring in the Pentagon and, again, what may be for one of them a half-mile walk is for the Secretary's special assistant merely a step across the hall.

This geography, incidentally, creates a continuous hassle over office space. The Secretary of Defense is located in room 3 E 880; that is, room 880, on the third floor, in ring E. Because of the pyramidal power structure we've been discussing, few Pentagon officials volunteer for offices in, say, room 100 on the fifth floor in ring A. Everyone wants to be next door to the Secretary. As it happens, there is a way in which this could be accomplished.

The Pentagon is basically a five-story building with offices on each floor strung out along five parallel corridors numbered A, B, C, D, and E. Think of it as a pond into which you have just dropped a stone. The ripple nearest the center is ring A; the one farthest out is ring E.

In the middle of all this, at the precise point where you dropped the stone, is an area of grass and shrubs surrounding a large wooden hot-dog stand. One need not be a geometrician to see that this hot-dog stand is equidistant from more points in the Pentagon than any other—and is therefore the logical place to put the Secretary of Defense. My failure to get him relocated, in spite of conclusive demonstrations that it is the optimum solution to the status problems of Pentagon officials, is merely one more example of how hard it is to impose a creative idea on the federal bureaucracy.

There is, of course, still another pyramid which rests upon all the departments of the government, known as the White House. Your role as a special assistant to a member of the cabinet is to protect him against White House special assistants, and even against the President, until such time as you succeed in becoming a special assistant to the President yourself, thus entering at long last into the inner mysteries of King Tut's tomb.

There is no firm formula for making this last, most important transition. A good way to begin is to persuade your Secretary that he needs a "single focal point of communication with the White House" and that this focal point should be you.

MEMORANDUM
TO: The Secretary
FROM: The Special Assistant
SUBJECT: White House Communications

At the last staff meeting you protested (quite rightly, in my opinion) about the continuing confusion in our day-to-day communications with members of the White House staff. I thoroughly concur with your instructions that an information memo be filed with you by any member of the staff who has spoken to a W.H. aide. There is considerable question in my mind, however, whether this will be sufficient to achieve the desired orderly procedure.

Therefore, I suggest the following: All direct W.H. telephone lines will be removed except those in your own office, so that members of the W.H. staff wishing to contact this Department will automatically reach this office. Most such calls, of course, concern routine matters with which you need not become involved. If you approve, I will undertake to screen all such contacts, referring to you those which are of Secretarial significance and passing on to other members of the Department requests properly concerning their duties.

The advantage to such an arrangement is that it gives us an on-going log of all W.H. contacts at the time they occur and also of the follow-up, since all actions taken will have to be reported back to the W.H. through my office. I believe this will eliminate most if not all of the confusion and complaints we have been getting from the President.

——APPROVED
——DISAPPROVED

If you can get your Secretary's initials in the approved box of this memo, you are on your way to the White House. Your name will embellish every memo the Presi-

dent sees from your Department, other than those from the
Secretary himself. His curiosity will be aroused. And,
since Presidents are invariably short-handed for good executive assistants, you may count on hearing from him.

What to Do When You Get to the White House

THE LATE HUMORIST Will Cuppy once urged
us to count among our blessings the fact that it is no longer
necessary for anybody to rise at 5 A.M. to go watch Louis
XIV put on his pants. He obviously knew nothing about
the White House. To be the first man the President sees
when he wakes up in the morning and/or the last he sees
before closing his eyes at night is the mark of final success
in Washington, surpassed only by actually being President
oneself, if then. Since the President normally sleeps in his
own bedroom (The Secret Service leaves him little choice),
the man who spoke to the President last is most likely to be
the one who has just come from "the family quarters."

What transpires in the bedroom, what is actually said
to you by the President, is of no real importance.

One special assistant was once praised by his President
in a news conference with these words: "He was late for
work this morning for the first time. He got in after the sun
had been up and had to go pull the curtain, with the sun
shining in my eyes. He is usually there early."

In Washington, a man can dine out on that kind of
encomium for months. Far more important is the fact that

you are free for the rest of the day to begin conversations with "The President told me in the bedroom this morning . . ." Most senior White House assistants consider this well worth getting up early for.

One piece of reliable advice I should be able to give you in return for your having paid the purchase price of this book is the answer to the question "How do I get into the President's bedroom?" I cannot honestly answer this question because I never made it. I did, however, once stand outside the President's bedroom door while the game was played, and was deeply impressed.

A few of us had just finished a late working lunch in the President's private dining room, after which it was his intention to take a nap. (I would be equally suspicious of any President who failed to work through lunch and one who failed to nap afterward; after all, your average President has gone to a great deal of trouble to earn the privilege of working at home and this is certainly one of the major fringe benefits.) Our business was clearly finished when the President rose from the table but, since we had not been specifically dismissed, we (I believe there were five of us) strolled with the President from the dining room to the door of his bedroom. En route, a very senior member of the staff, whom I shall call SA#1, contrived to open a new line of conversation which, as he had correctly calculated, made it necessary for him to accompany the President through the open door to the bedroom.

This left four of us outside, two, including myself, much too new to the game even to realize that a game was in progress, much less join it. The gambit was, however, instantly clear to SA#2. As I recall the event, he seems to be literally teetering on the balls of his feet, like an athlete waiting for the starter's gun, but this is probably an exaggeration of memory. Certainly he was engaged in the emotional equivalent of such action. During the microsecond it took him to reach a decision, I would suppose some such thought as this must have flickered across his mind:

"This conversation has absolutely nothing to do with me. . . . If I go in there and the President asks me what the hell *I* want, it could be embarrassing. . . . On the other hand, if I don't go in I'll have to listen to that conniving little S.O.B. tell lies for the rest of the afternoon about what the Boss said to him. . . ."

He opted for the immediate risk rather than the longer-term certainty and plunged through the door. Meanwhile, SA#3 had also been assessing the situation and was already leaning forward. But he was too slow, and SA#2 was by far the shrewder player. As SA#2 moved through the doorway he reached aside with the fingertips of his right hand and, with a barely perceptible flick of the wrist, gently closed the door to the President's bedroom in the face of his charging colleague.

It will not, I'm sure, surprise the reader to learn that SA#2 survived long after #1 and #3 had vanished into the pages of history—if, indeed, they are to be found even there.

In the White House, like the Pentagon, proximity to power is essential; and here, unlike the Pentagon, the problem cannot be resolved by moving the Chief to a hot-dog stand.

The operative rule is: *A closet in the West Wing is better than a three-room suite anyplace else.* In my time there was a junior assistant who did moderately well by rejecting all offers of luxurious accommodations in either the Executive Office Building or the East Wing and settling, when all else failed, for a portion of the ladies' room in the West Basement.

Former Congressman Brooks Hays, who shared the East Wing of the White House with Arthur Schlesinger during the Kennedy years ("I think the President keeps me there in case Arthur ever gets any really *hard* questions"), used to tell friends who asked whether he was close to the President: "Politically and philosophically, yes. Geographically, I am somewhat like the lady back in my old Congressional district who was pointed out to me as being nearly a hundred years old. I went up to her and asked, 'Did you see Halley's comet?'

" 'Only from a distance,' she said, 'only from a distance.' "

The moral is, get as close to the top of the pyramid as possible, but remember: the base of the White House still rests on top of all the other pyramids of power. The lowliest member of the White House staff, so long as his name is listed on the White House switchboard, has all the power he needs to impress his whims on the rest of the government, the country, and possibly even the world. A call from the White House is not a call from the East Wing, the West Wing, or the E.O.B.: it is a call from the White House. (Except to very senior career civil servants, which is one reason why you should never presume to call one. Stick to the cabinet secretaries and *their* special assistants— nearly all of them will be long gone from the government before they really understand the game.)

Call your cabinet officers directly, and preferably late at night. If the Secretary is not in his office, tell the White House operator to reach him at home.

"Mr. Secretary, this is Julien Sorel, at the White House. I'm glad to find you still in the office."

"I'm not still in the office, Mr. Sorel, I'm at home. In bed. With my wife. But what can I do for you?"

"I'm terribly sorry, Mr. Secretary. I guess the President just assumed that you, of all people, would still be working. At any rate, just before the President went to bed he asked me to tell you that he would like to see that residual fuel-oil report first thing in the morning."

"Just a minute, young man. You may not be aware of it, but I have a specific understanding with the President that I'm to get my marching instructions from him and nobody else."

"I understand that, Mr. Secretary. After all, you are a member of the cabinet. All I can tell you is that when the President was putting on his pajamas a few minutes ago, he *did* ask me to call you, and he *did* say he'd like to have the report first thing in the morning. He's probably asleep by now, but if you'd like me to awaken him . . ."

"Look . . . Julien . . . I haven't had any sleep for eighteen hours. I'll get him the damned report. But do you think it *has* to be first thing in the morning? How about sometime in the afternoon?"

"Mr. Secretary—Bob—I'm reasonably sure I can stall him until lunch. If the question comes up, I'll tell him the messenger is en route."

"Julien, thank you—and I won't forget this."

With this dialogue, you have won the first round of Who Talked to the President Last? You have established your position within the Pyramid Club.

But—be careful. Winning the game against mere cabinet officers is a far cry from outmaneuvering your colleagues on the White House staff. As remarked earlier, it is the difference between checkers and chess. Every practitioner will have to make his own clinical decisions, based on the situations he encounters—which will differ in significant detail from one administration to another. President Nixon, for example, is maintaining a private study in the E.O.B., which may mean that in *this* administration the E.O.B. is not necessarily Siberia. Some future President may enjoy the view from the East Wing, and that, again, will change the details. The fundamentals will remain.

Your greatest temptation will be to overplay your hand. This, in fact, is what ultimately happened to my colleague who talked his way into the President's bedroom after that lunch. Power went to his head. He became so confident that he left standing instructions with his secretary to tell all callers with whom he did not wish to speak: "I'm sorry, Sir, but he's with the President." This eventually created an opportunity for another and wiser assistant to respond, "I don't know who *his* President is, but *my* President is standing right here—and would like very much to talk to him."

Sic transit gloria mundi.

And well it should—as some day I'm sure you'll agree; but probably not yet.

5

Broad Jumping the Credibility Gap
And, How to Make the Sawdust Softer on Your Side

To write news in its perfection requires such a combination of qualities that a man completely fitted for the task is not always to be found. In Sir Henry Wotton's jocular definition, an ambassador is said to be a man of virtue sent abroad to tell lies for the advantage of his country; a newswriter is a man without virtue, who writes lies at home for his own profit. To these compositions is required neither genius or knowledge, neither industry nor sprightliness; but contempt of shame and indifference to truth are absolutely necessary. He who by a long familiarity with infamy has obtained these qualities, may confidently tell today what he intends to contradict tomorrow; he may affirm fearlessly what he knows that he shall be obliged to recant, and may write letters from Amsterdam or Dresden to himself. —SAMUEL JOHNSON

THIS ESTIMATE, predating the birth of the American Republic and authored by the inventor of the dictionary, nicely summarizes the establishment view of journalists in all times and places. God knows what Dr. Johnson would have thought about television commentators, but one suspects that he would not have been unkind to Spiro Agnew.

There is no need to recite the common opinion of the Fourth Estate concerning the Establishment. It can be heard any afternoon at the bar of the National Press Club. Having served on both sides of the credibility gap (as well as being passing familiar with the aforementioned saloon) I am obliged to suggest that both parties just might be right.

That there is some affinity between government and the press is shown by the ease with which Washington reporters step into government jobs and former officials become successful columnists. Moreover, viewpoints are remarkably interchangeable. Before he was appointed Assistant Secretary of Defense for Public Affairs, for example, my good friend Arthur Sylvester was manager of the Washington bureau of the Newark *News* with a twenty-five-year reputation as an uncompromising capital news hound. In his official capacity, he soon found himself under vociferous attack by his former colleagues as the inventor of "managed news" and "the government's right to lie."

The tension between reporters and politicians is like the competition between pedestrians and motorists: you swear at the careless pedestrians up to the moment you find a parking space, then you curse the reckless drivers. And who is to say you are wrong in either instance?

Former Secretary of Labor Willard Wirtz, in a speech at the Overseas Press Club, once suggested "A Pure Speech and Press Law" to afford the consumer the same protection against what goes into his head that he now receives on behalf of his stomach.

Thus, speeches would include a note at the beginning:

Not written by the speaker. Prepared for another occasion and altered to fit this audience. All classical references taken from Bartlett's *Familiar Quotations* or Elbert Hubbard's *Scrap-*

book. All statistics conveniently adjusted. . . . Shake head well after hearing.

Similarly, there would be a compulsory box at the head of the next day's report of the speech, reading something like this:

> Written by Jones, who wasn't present, from ticker item filed by Smith, who wasn't there either. All quotes from speech taken out of context. Reported crowd reactions, including pickets, dubbed in. Headline written by Shrudlu, who can count but cannot read English. Dangerous if taken seriously or without a large grain of salt.

Honest men who have served in what the Rand Corporation would call the "interface" between government and the press must admit that the public often has ample grounds to wish a plague on both our houses. A few years ago, for example, the United States was engaged in certain military activities in Thailand related to the war in Vietnam which the government was—to say the least—not anxious to publicize.

Word of the troop buildup, etc., did get to the American people as more and more correspondents filed dispatches from Bangkok. This tribute to the perspicacity of a free press would be somewhat more impressive, however, if the plethora of reports out of Thailand had not happened to coincide with the accompanying buildup there of wives and dependents of Vietnam-based correspondents, who were understandably anxious for excuses to file a first-hand report.

In the same vein, Lyndon Johnson, urged on by the Secret Service, may have been unduly secretive in his travel plans. But a surprising amount of the press protest over that secrecy resulted from irritation on the part of members of the White House press corps over their problem in deciding whether to plan a Saturday-night dinner party in Washington or to get out their golf clubs for a weekend in Austin.

The casting of stones, however, is traditionally reserved for those who are without sin. All that remains to me, I fear, is to offer a few hints about how to play this particular game for the benefit of those colleagues who insist on rushing in where angels fear to tread—a familiar compulsion for journalists of almost every clime and condition of servitude.

For the purpose of this discussion, we will assume that you are about to accept a reporting job in Washington. (If you are already in the government and contemplate journalism as a postwar career, the lessons will be useful later; in the interim, they may help protect you from your future colleagues.)

Your first problem is to decide what kind of political journalist you intend to be. Although there is, naturally, a certain amount of overlap between categories, every Washington commentator must basically choose to be (a) a Spy, (b) a Thinker, or (c) a Spokesman. There is also a fourth category, known as Washington humor, but, as Art Buchwald has pointed out, he and Joe Alsop have this specialty pretty well locked up.

The Spy

THIS IS Washington's nearest approximation to what is known elsewhere as "straight reporting." No one can make a living reporting "the facts" from Washington because the agency press releases are more than sufficient to fill every daily newspaper in the country three times over.

What the Spy specializes in is inside information. He may get every bit of it from the mimeographed handouts, but no matter. The Spy's trade consists not so much in reporting the news as describing how the news was created, and by whom. This requires not so much legwork as a fruitful imagination—and some occasional fast footwork when a particular inside story falls apart.

A common example is what I like to think of as a post hoc riposte to a prediction gone wrong. On Monday, let us say, you have informed millions of your readers that "after weeks of delay, caused principally by intense and occasionally strident debate within the administration, the President has finally decided on a candidate to fill the long-vacant post of Assistant Secretary of State for Negotiating with the Pentagon. He is Congressman Joe Smith, Republican from Idaho."

On Tuesday, the President announces the appointment. It is Rabbi Isadore Finestein of Cleveland, Ohio.

The lead for your Wednesday column is automatic. "Outraged at what he called 'premature press leaks,' an angry President yesterday abruptly canceled plans to appoint Rep. Joe Smith (R.), Idaho, to a key post in the State Department. White House aides involved in the decision confide, off the record, that they themselves were taken by complete surprise by the President's action, which some attribute to an item which appeared in this column on Monday. . . ."

You will be surprised at how many editors around the country are willing to buy this kind of copy.

For the television commentator, the equivalent technique involves delivering his nightly commentary from the north lawn of the White House with the door to the West Basement or the North Portico serving as background. The copy may have been written at the office, or rewritten off the A.P. wire on the way to the White House, but that background guarantees authenticity. So cameramen, sound men, and network correspondents will contrive to stand in the sleet and snow of a Washington winter or the steamroom humidity of a Washington summer to preserve that all-important symbol. There is technically no reason, of course, why the scene couldn't be painted on a backdrop in the studio, but this would doubtless violate the truth-in-broadcasting codes.

Lest I seem to be losing my impartiality and offering too much help to the working press and not enough to their natural enemies, let us pause for a moment to look at the event from the viewpoint of a government official. Suppose Congressman Joe Smith is, in fact, the last man in the world you'd like to see in that job. Suppose also that Joe has so much political clout in the Congress that he just must be considered. And suppose, finally, that the President has a well-known aversion to press announcements of his forthcoming appointments before he is ready to announce them. What would *you* do? (If you have to think before answering, you are wasting the taxpayers' money and should resign from the government.)

It was the Duke of Wellington who, upon being approached by a stranger who greeted him with "Mr. Smith, I believe," responded: "If you believe *that*, Sir, you will believe anything."

For reasons beyond the control of everybody, I fear we must continue to apply that dictum to those innocent souls—be they reporters, editors, readers, or viewers—who persist in believing that they are somehow getting "inside information" out of Washington. (There is reason to suspect that the same is true of foreign intelligence agencies who send *real* spys to Washington, but that is outside the scope of our essay.)

As Lyndon Johnson once remarked about a now long-forgotten "leak" of allegedly inside information, "I saw the story and I would say that [it] probably represents a highly aggressive reporter who met a man who wanted to appear smart."

The Thinker

IT HAS BEEN SUGGESTED that there is so little humorous copy out of Washington because there is nothing funny about what goes on there. A similar principle, perhaps, would explain why there are currently so few Washington newsmen who specialize in "thinking," once the prized domain of the aristocrats of political journalism.

What are the qualifications of a Thinking Washington newsman? To gain wide acceptance the Thinker must possess what we may call the three A's: age, apathy, and arrogance.

Age, popularly associated with wisdom, is hard to acquire except through patience. You can bleach your hair and walk with a scholarly stoop, but—unless you were born abroad in a country which has since gone out of business—the birth registrars and the obit writers will sooner or later discover your secret. We must reluctantly conclude, therefore, that Thinker is no job for the beginner. He will find it advisable to begin as a Spy and work his way up slowly, possibly with a short stint as a Spokesman (*q.v.*) in between.

Apathy, to the Thinker, is the proper response to the hysteria of the times—such as nuclear missiles in Cuba or people burning down forty square blocks of Washington. This kind of thing is for night city editors and cub reporters. It is the Thinker's job to sit in a cork-lined room with a copy of Walter Pater, the works of Macaulay, and a set of the Great Books, meditating about what it all means.

The Thinking Washington correspondent's chief problem is *style*. I once knew a young reporter whose ambition, he said, was "to think like Walter Lippmann and write like Murray Kempton." There could hardly be a more magnificent step in the wrong direction. For the Thinker, true success consists in predictions reminiscent of the more obscure prophecies of the Delphic Oracle and Nostradamus.

In the good old days—whenever that was—the Thinker was expected to pick up where the Spy left off. Thus, your colleague having established the facts of the Congressman v. the Rabbi imbroglio, it would be your business to observe:

The continuing crisis of decision within the present administration, not to mention the ambivalence within the President's own mind—the existence of which has become increasingly suspected and deplored by thoughtful observers—has finally surfaced in the growing controversy over White House handling of the extremely delicate competition for a high government post between partisans of a powerful Congressman and a distinguished member of the clergy; indeed, there are those who believe that, thanks to staff indecisiveness and Presidential ambivalence, there has now been introduced into an already explosive situation, tragically and gratuitously, a fundamental Constitutional question going to the heart of the First Amendment concerning separation of Church and State.

That lead is, I confess, a pale imitation of what would be produced by a real professional, but it does contain the essential elements: it is all one sentence and tells us absolutely nothing of substance, including the true opinions of the author.

Arrogance, the third A, represents the Thinker's principal advantage in Washington: his insulation from the game of Who Talked to the President Last? To the Spy or the Spokesman, non-access to the President is a serious handicap which must be overcome by a continuous fox trot of fast footwork; to the Thinker, never speaking to the President can be a positive advantage. In fact, one of the principal requirements of a successful Thinker is the arrogance to refuse phone calls from the President of the United States, and to turn down all invitations to White House receptions. A dean of the profession ultimately moved out of Washington, leaving behind a farewell letter explaining that his many friendships among Washington officialdom, including the President, had begun to compromise his objectivity.

That is the only way to play it—but, as previously noted, it is not a game for the neophyte.

The Spokesman

THE FINAL CATEGORY is a Washington specialization which is at once the easiest to perform, the hardest to enter, and the most insecure. It consists of being—entirely by rumor—the informal Spokesman for the Establishment. In other words, combining in one person the function traditionally performed by the *Times* of London for the government over there, and which used to be performed by the *New York Times* for the government over here.

In modern Washington, being Spokesman for the Establishment means essentially having the President's ear. It implies a first-name relationship with the Chief Executive

which can only result from long friendship. Charles Bartlett had it during the Kennedy Administration and, to a
somewhat lesser extent, William S. White in the Johnson
Administration. Bartlett's claim arose from the widely held
belief that he was the man who introduced John Kennedy
to Jacqueline; White's from the fact that he and LBJ were
the same age and emigrated from Texas to Washington together.

A normal lead for the Spokesman will begin:

> Despite those who claim to know best, including the White
> House staff and key members of the cabinet, the President has
> no intention of intervening in the current three-way dispute
> between the State Department and the Pentagon, on the one
> hand, and the House Armed Services Committee on the other.
> Indeed, the President has many private reservations about the
> efficacy of both his Secretary of State and his Secretary of
> Defense. If the controversy continues, some observers would
> not be surprised to see a reshuffling of the Cabinet. . . .

The voice is Jacob's, but the hand is the hand of Esau.
The danger is that Esau may withdraw his hand at any
moment—and where does that leave Jacob? It was suggested to John Kennedy at a White House press conference
that Mr. Bartlett's article in the *Satevepost* was being given
undue weight because of his presumed friendship with the
President, and what did Mr. Kennedy intend to do about
that? (An example, incidentally, of the friendship and
camaraderie which may be expected from one's journal-
istic colleagues in Washington.) President Kennedy bailed
out Mr. Bartlett by saying that the White House is a very

poor place to make friends and that he intended to keep the ones he already had. But suppose he had said, instead, *"Who* is Charles Bartlett?"

To be a Spokesman is, in short, to add additional insecurity to an already insecure profession. Furthermore it requires a close relationship with the incumbent prior to his becoming the Maximum Leader—and this depends on luck. I cannot recommend it.

Reference was made earlier to the ease with which Washington newsmen drift into government, and government officials become syndicated columnists. If you are contemplating a Washington career, either in or out of government, you would do well to study these transactions. However mysterious they may seem—how did Hearst ever get an important man like that? why would a crusading reporter sell out to the Pentagon?—such transformations really come down to money.

In an address to the Newspaper Publishers Association, President Kennedy once said:

"You may remember that in 1851, the New York Herald Tribune, under the sponsorship and publishing of Horace Greeley, employed as its London correspondent an obscure journalist by the name of Karl Marx.

"We are told that foreign correspondent Marx, stone broke, and with a family ill and undernourished, constantly appealed to Greeley and Managing Editor Charles Dana for an increase in his munificent salary of $5 per installment, a salary which he and Engels ungratefully labeled as the 'lousiest petty bourgeois cheating.'

"But when all his financial appeals were refused, Marx looked around for other means of livelihood and fame, eventually terminating his relationship with the Tribune and devoting his talents full time to the cause that would bequeath to the world the seeds of Leninism, Stalinism, revolution and the cold war.

"If only this capitalistic New York newspaper had treated him more kindly; if only Marx had remained a foreign correspondent, history might have been different. And I hope all publishers will bear this lesson in mind the next time they receive a poverty-stricken appeal for a small increase in the expense account from an obscure newspaper man."

There is no evidence that any publisher then present took positive action as a result of the President's remarks. Consequently, every nonsyndicated reporter may at any time be seduced away from the practice of journalism by an invitation to become Assistant Secretary of Something-or-other at a salary increase of five to ten thousand dollars. Similarly, senior officials may be bought by the syndicate for an even larger increment of income.

As citizens, we should no doubt deplore all this. As workingmen trying to make a living, we must at least understand how the system works.

It helps to know that both officialdom and pressdom have always exaggerated their own importance. As James Bryce wrote back in 1893, in answer to the suggestion that the best Americans do not go into politics because of their fear of what was then known as a licentious press: "No more there than in Europe has any upright man been written down, for though the American press is unsparing, the American people are shrewd, and sometimes believe too little rather than too much evil of a man whom the press assails."

A century before Bryce, Benjamin Franklin, that wise old man who knew something about everything including government and the newspaper business, offered everyone a compromise: "If by the liberty of the press, we understand merely the liberty of discussing the propriety of public measures and political opinions, let us have as much of it as you please; but, if it means the liberty of affronting, calumniating, and defaming one another, I own myself willing to part with my share of it whenever our legislators shall please to alter the law; and shall cheerfully consent to exchange my liberty of abusing others for the privilege of not being abused myself."

Poor Ben. This is exactly the kind of provocation one would expect from a man foolish enough to fly kites in a thunderstorm. He always was out of step with his times and, it becomes increasingly obvious, never is going to catch up.

6

The Honorable Man in Business
and Academia

Not because of any extraordinary talents did he succeed, but because he had a capacity for business and not above it. —TACITUS

OUR CLOSING PAGES will be devoted to advising Presidents of the United States, actual or prospective, about how to protect themselves from some of the phenomena we've witnessed. If the President will be patient for just a few more moments, however, I think it only fair to offer a brief warning to such lesser executives as, say, the president of General Motors, who often find themselves similarly besieged. For, unlike old soldiers, old cabinet officers and aging special assistants do not just fade away—they "return to private industry." At least three cabinet officers from my own administration became partners in Wall Street investment houses, and the Dow-Jones industrials dropped 185 points in the ensuing twelve months. Unfortunately, I made the mistake of going with them, which might not have happened had I enjoyed the benefit of the advice you are getting now.

When the late Herbert Bayard Swope was editor of the New York *World*, legend has it that he concluded interviews with aspiring reporters by asking, "Young man, are you a graduate of any accredited school of journalism?" Only if the answer was "No" did the young man get the job. "The problem with schools of journalism," Swope said, "is that the only thing they teach you is how to be managing editor. What I need is reporters. This paper already has a managing editor. Me."

A similar incapacity for laboring at life's lesser chores is likely to afflict the returned public official. Even though he may be coming back to the firm he left at the beginning of his Washington career, you will find that he is not the same man. He has been manipulating the levers of power on the most awesome political juggernaut in history; it will be hard to immerse himself in your next year's advertising campaign. Furthermore, he has become accustomed to rounding off the numbers on his expense account to the nearest billion dollars. And, if he worked in the White House, he has probably forgotten how to make a phone call.

The latter disability results from the fact that the White House telephone operators constitute the best organized, most competent group of ladies in the capital and possibly on earth. Once set in pursuit of a quarry, they will follow him electronically to the gates of hell, if need be, and perhaps beyond. They are rumored to be able even to penetrate the intricate mysteries of the telephone system of New York City. During President Johnson's trip to Asia in 1966, his principal foreign-affairs advisor, Walt Rostow, disappeared for a time in the labyrinth of the Hotel Manila. All efforts by the staff, the Secret Service, and

the Philippine security forces failed to locate him. In a moment of inspiration, I picked up one of the direct lines which the Army Signal Corps had strung between the President's suite and the White House. "Where," I asked the operator, "is Mr. Rostow?"

"He's supposed to be with all of you in Manila," she replied.

"I know. But we can't find him."

"Just a moment, sir. I'll try to locate him."

My recollection is that we were speaking to Mr. Rostow from some obscure wing of the hotel, via the White House, in something under two minutes.

This sort of convenience, like instant takeoffs in Air Force One while everybody else in the country stays grounded, can be terribly demoralizing. You are going to have much difficulty fitting the man who has experienced it back into your organization. The safer course would be simply not to hire him or, if he happens to come from the education business, refuse to restore his faculty tenure. There has been some tendency in this direction recently, but I'm afraid it can't be recommended. Plato tells us that "the punishment suffered by the wise who refuse to take part in the government is to live under the government of bad men." If every Cambridge professor who accepts the call to Washington must anticipate being exiled to some state university in the provinces when his tour of duty ends, the resulting situation will be even less agreeable than what we have now. It will be equally bad if corporate vice-presidents find themselves unemployable in the advertising game after working for the Federal Trade Commission.

No, if the American system is to survive, these people must be permitted to come home again after performing what most of them sincerely believe to be their civic duty. The problem is that they are not at all like our elderly parents or grandparents, who can be settled in a nursing home or retirement village. Despite the atrophy of such minor skills as dialing a telephone or driving one's own automobile, these are German police dogs trained in twenty-seven varieties of mayhem who, now that the war is over, must be taught to live harmlessly with children. (If you think it naïve to compare the executive suite or the humanities faculty at Harvard with a children's nursery, you should return to GO and read this book all over again. Alternatively, you may learn the same lesson by employing an unreconditioned Washington special assistant and giving him the office next door.)

Someday, perhaps, the government will provide the same sort of debriefing facilities to departing officials it provides for Air Force pilots returning from bombing missions or that the Army furnished for retiring "war dogs" after the Second World World War. Meanwhile, we shall have to do the best we can within the private sector. Here are some suggestions.

The Initial Interview (Commercial)

AFTER he has moved into his new office, you will want to drop in on the returned veteran and converse with him along the following lines—your purpose being to remind him that life in what he now thinks of as "the outside" is different from life on "the inside."

"Joe, it's good to have you back."

"It's good to be back, my friend." (Before Washington, he might have said "sir.")

"I like your office. And all those autographed pictures of the President certainly can't hurt the company's image. Too bad he wasn't reelected."

"Well, he was a great man and I'll always be proud of having worked for him."

"Of course you will, Joe. And I want you to know that the company was proud of *you*, all those years in Washington. You did a great job down there—whatever it was you were doing."

"Thank you."

"Joe, looking at these pictures gives me an idea. You remember the bonuses we give out every Christmas?"

"I certainly do. They've always been very generous."

"Yes—and they also cost the company a hell of a lot of money. Based on your Washington experience, what would you say if this year we eliminated the cash and just passed out some autographed pictures? Maybe a picture of the chairman for the vice-presidents and one of me for the employees."

Joe (*after long pause*): "Well . . . I'm not entirely sure that would . . . satisfy the help."

"I'm not either. But you might think about it."

With a little bit of luck, this colloquy will set Joe to

thinking about such dull matters as cash flow, profit and loss, liquidity, and all the other mundane matters to which government is essentially immune. Ultimately, he will come to realize that getting money is no longer a simple matter of outarguing the Budget director or outsmarting the House Appropriations Committee. (This step may be omitted if you are a railroad, telephone company, light or gas company, bank, insurance company, or Defense Department contractor.)

The Initial Interview (*Academic*)

THE ACADEMIC VERSION of the initial interview for our returning veteran might proceed somewhat as follows. Let us assume that you are chairman of the Political Science Department and he has been appointed Roving Professor of Contemporary Government.

"It's good to see you again, Joseph. We followed your adventures in Washington with more than academic interest."

"Why, thank you. It was certainly a stimulating experience, although I don't really claim to have accomplished much."

"Oh, nobody is blaming *you* for anything, Joseph. Well, there was some static from a few of the younger faculty when they heard you were coming back, but I'm sure that when they get to know you they'll realize you had very little to say about what went on down there."

"Well, now, I'm not trying to *disclaim* responsibility.

Actually, I was very closely involved with events, and I'm not ashamed of anything."

"Of course you're not, Joseph. None of us would have expected you to be. We've known you for a long time. What does concern me, though, is that you've been away from the field for rather a long while."

"I beg your pardon?"

"The thing is, Joseph, that—speaking frankly—political science has come a long way while you were down in Washington and it's going to take you a while to catch up. We want to make it as easy for you as possible, so I've assigned you to teach Government 101. It's only two hours a week and you'll be dealing only with freshmen. I'm sure you can handle it, and still have plenty of time to catch up on your reading."

A Distinction Without a Difference

ALL SUCH EFFORTS to provide decompression of the ego for "returning" public officials are acts of charity and should be tax deductible. But, while a kindness to the recipient, and a form of self-protection for the benefactor, such aids to readjustment are becoming less and less necessary—for the difference between a corporate, university, or government bureaucracy is one of the few differences among men we seem to be successfully eliminating. There is a reason for this, and it is not terribly complicated. In organizations, as in architecture, form follows function—and also the lack of it. It was, in fact, clearly foreseen by the father of our economic system in the year of our national independence. In *The Wealth of Nations*, published in 1776, Adam Smith tells us:

The labour of some of the most respectable orders in the society is, like that of menial servants, unproductive of any value, and does not fix or realize itself in any permanent subject, or vendible commodity, which endures after that labour is past, and for which an equal quantity of labour could afterwards be procured. The sovereign, for example, with all the officers both of justice and war who serve under him, the whole army and navy, are unproductive labourers. They are the servants of the public, and are maintained by a part of the annual produce of the industry of other people. Their service, how honourable, how useful, or how necessary soever, produces nothing for which an equal quantity of service can afterwards be procured. The protection, security, and defence of the commonwealth, the effect of their labour this year, will not purchase its protection, security, and defence for the year to come. In the same class must be ranked, some both of the gravest and most important, and some of the most frivolous professions: churchmen, lawyers, physicians, men of letters of all kinds; players, buffoons, musicians, opera-singers, opera-dancers, etc. The labour of the meanest of these has a certain value, regulated by the very same principles which regulate that of every other sort of labour; and that of the noblest and most useful, produces nothing which could afterwards purchase or procure an equal quantity of labour. Like the declamation of the actor, the harangue of the orator, or the tune of the musician, the work of all of them perishes in the very instant of its production.

Let him who is without sin cast the first stone. Meanwhile, let us see what can be done to help our senior colleague, the President of the United States.

7

How to Survive Although President
of the United States

*A king may be a tool, a thing of straw; but if he serves to frighten
our enemies, and secure our property, it is well enough; a scarecrow is
a thing of straw, but it protects the corn.* —ALEXANDER POPE

THESE FINAL WORDS will be of interest only to
those who are, or expect to be, President of the United
States. All others will kindly avert their eyes.

Mr. President, we promised in the beginning to help
you avoid the mistakes of President Monroe. His problem,
you will recall, was failure to appreciate Jefferson's warning about cormorants.

Generically, Mr. Monroe's problem was no different
from that of every other ruler, including Our Savior, who
had a disciple named Judas. "The first mistake a ruler
makes," said Machiavelli, "is usually in the selection of his
staff." There is, he observed, a sound and universal rule for
judging the qualities of an assistant. "If a ruler sees his
servant considering his own position before his master's,
trying to derive personal benefits from administrative action, he is a bad minister and of doubtful loyalty. The man
responsible for the exercise of a ruler's power should have

no thoughts for any other's but his master's advantage, least of all his own, nor any concern but his master's."

Machiavelli wrote all this, of course, in a book designed to persuade Lorenzo de'Medici to give him a government job. But his recommendations for achieving this happy relationship between the ruler and his staff are so inadequate that we can easily understand why Lorenzo never gave him an appointment.

Jefferson had the key in that reference to cormorants and it is truly a shame President Monroe failed to pick it up.

There is rarely much you can do about the Congress, Mr. President, and even less about those ingrates you appointed to the Supreme Court. But members of the Executive Branch are supposed to work for *you*. True, you aren't really allowed to order around members of the career Civil Service, the Foreign Service, or the professional military. (My publisher finds this hard to believe and we had an argument over the statement; but you and I know the truth, don't we, Sir?) Yet the political appointees—including not only the cabinet officers but even members of the White House staff—are morally obliged to pay some attention to your wishes. Furthermore, you are legally and morally entitled to enforce your desires with these people. It is all a matter of knowing how. And that is where the cormorants come in.

A cormorant, Mr. President, is a particularly noisy and unkempt bird which nests along the sea coast and lives on fish. It is a great diver and can seize a fish from the bottom of a pool or stream in a matter of seconds. In ancient times they were used for fishing—the trick being to fasten a ring or strap around the bird's neck, loose enough to let him breathe but tight enough to keep him from swallowing the fish. The only other equipment required was a face mask worn by the owner to protect himself from the bird's beak on the way to the beach.

There you have it, Mr. President. All the cormorants described in these pages, and all the rest we never got around to, can be put to productive use—provided only that you find the right kind of collar and never forget your face mask.

At the risk of seeming presumptuous, I will offer a few modest suggestions. These will be limited to how properly to throttle (a) the White House staff, (b) the cabinet, and (c) certain key members of the career civil service.

How to Control the White House

THE ESSENTIAL FACT to remember about the White House staff is that everyone there, with the possible exception of yourself, Mr. President, is there by accident. No one ever plans his career to include several years in the White House. He is always surprised to arrive.

When Joe Tumulty, that extraordinary professional Irish politician who made Woodrow Wilson President, entered the White House to take charge as Wilson's chief assistant, his first official act was to call his father in Jersey City and announce: "Well, Dad, I'm in the White House." (Entering the same place two generations later, I immedi-

ately wrote a letter to my mother—on White House sta-
tionery).

Everyone does something like this. The problem is
that the surprise quickly wears off. In a remarkably short
time your White House appointee will progress from awe
to a feeling of gratification that his own excellence has at
last been recognized and that he finally occupies his natural
place in life. Eventually he will begin to realize that, while
it is nice to be a Presidential assistant, there have been better
Presidents to assist than the one he happens to be stuck
with. At this point he will begin giving background brief-
ings to the press to prove that whatever is going wrong in
the White House is not *his* fault but—guess whose?

He has thrown off the collar and is fishing for himself.
That this requires befouling his own nest is no real obstacle
—the phrase was *invented* to describe the habits of the
cormorant.

Now, how do we control this? How do we tighten the
collar? The answer, Mr. President, is absurdly simple. You
must, personally, control assignments to the White House
mess, office space, telephone service, access to White House
limousines, and invitations to White House receptions and
dinners. *Under no circumstances should these powers be
delegated.* They are really your only tools for controlling
the egocentric—and extremely powerful—bunch of cormorants who constitute your staff.

You have no way of knowing from experience, Mr.
President, because you have never served on the White
House staff. Since the last of our Founding Fathers died,

no one who ever worked in the White House has gone on to become President, nor ever will—for the same reason that Premier Stalin's private secretary, Mr. Malenkov, was unable to stand up to Mr. Khrushchev. These are hothouse plants, Mr. President, however brilliant their foliage, and the way to handle them is to control their environment. (I'm sorry about mixing these metaphors, but the point is clearer this way.)

The White House environment consists mainly of the aforementioned perquisites. These are, after all, people who daily stand before kings, or at least speak to them on the telephone, in your name. If *you* don't control them, no one will. And there is nothing more astonishing to a man so situated than to be suddenly moved from group two to group one in the White House mess (the Armed Forces aide will be happy to explain this to you), or to be suddenly denied limousine service. Mr. President, *the man who controls these perquisites controls the White House staff—and that man should be the President, not some power-hungry executive assistant.*

Your fundamental strategy should be to keep everyone around you off balance. To this end you must frequently shuffle not only their privileges and office space but also their psychic images of themselves. Keep track of your appointments, noting carefully who on the staff seems to be talking to you most. The *dramatis personae* around the oval office shifts almost imperceptibly but, if one watches the faces attentively, much can be learned about who is doing what to whom in which part of the jungle.

You have, let us say, a personal assistant named Zimmerman. During the first months of your administration he seemed to be standing around every corner you turned, from the rose garden to the men's room in the basement; lately, however, he has been appearing less and less often at all the important meetings. When you inquire about him, some other aide mutters vaguely that "he's working on that research project with the Budget people." This translates as "We've got the bastard locked up in the Executive Office Building and if I have *my* way you'll never set eyes on him again."

Zimmerman is obviously a current loser in the White House game. Your best response—after checking with the White House telephone operators to make sure Zimmerman is still alive—is to mention him to the next friendly newspaperman whom you deign to honor with an off-the-record chat. You will say, "I want to say—strictly off the record—that I am proud of my staff. I think I've got the best bunch of guys working for me of any President in this century—and the best of the bunch is probably young Zimmerman."

The reporter, of course, will immediately write a White House "backgrounder" about Zimmerman's rapidly rising star in your administration. Zimmerman will instantly start sending you memos again and nobody on the staff will have the nerve to sneak them out of your night reading. After a few days, call Zimmerman in for a conference. Show him the memos. "Zimmerman," you might say, "there are some pretty fair ideas in here. If you'd spend more time on things like this and less time getting your name in the newspapers, you might be very valuable around here." Having used Zimmerman to deflate everybody else, you have now shot down Zimmerman. Many variations of this move will easily occur to you—but it is most important that you do something of the sort at least once a week.

Keeping Your Back to the Wall in the Cabinet Room

FDR's Secretary of the Interior, Harold L. Ickes confided to his diary on July 21, 1936:

> I am really sorry now that I did not resign a year ago. I had a good issue then. When I was approached with the proposition that if I should resign there was a good chance that I might be nominated for President on the Republican ticket, I did not take it seriously. But one reason I did not consider it seriously was on account of my loyalty to the President. I could not see myself resigning from his Cabinet and then opposing him. I have never done that sort of thing. . . . On the other hand, Roosevelt . . . I am beginning to fear . . . is too sure of himself, too certain of his own judgement, and less and less willing to seek or take advice from competent men. To a diminishing extent does he confer with men of standing and substance. He is surrounding himself with men like Morgenthau and Hopkins and Tugwell, plus a lot of even lesser lights. I rather shudder to think of what his Cabinet will be during his next term if he is re-elected.

Not all cabinet officers keep diaries but if they did and you could read them, Mr. President, sooner or later you would encounter thoughts like these—and not just on one day of the year. There is something about being appointed to the cabinet which goes to a man's head. There is, as you undoubtedly know, Sir, a long-standing Washington custom that the cabinet never meets in the absence of the President except at his specific request. The reason is obvious. Insist that it be observed, or if, for some unaccountable reason, you are forced to let them convene without you, at least make certain that the Vice President doesn't get in.

Controlling them collectively will not suffice, however; you must also deal with them as individuals. This does not mean you have to talk to them or go fishing with them, or whatever. But it does mean that you cannot afford to lose track of any of them for any considerable time, or to lose sight of their respective strengths and weaknesses. If yours is an average cabinet, and most of them are, you will have one or two politicians, a couple of millionaires, an intellectual (or, rather, the kind of college professor who writes significant books and becomes chairman of his department, if not president of the university), and an old friend. Each of these gentlemen is susceptible to a different form of control, and each is dangerous in a special manner.

It should hardly be necessary to warn a man who has been in politics as long as you, Sir, that the most threatening of the lot is your old friend. When a man finds himself defending his freedom in a law court, it is rarely a total stranger who takes the witness stand for the prosecution. A friend, indeed, has been defined as a former stranger on the way to becoming an ingrate. This is nowhere so true as in the White House. The best way to deal with your old friend is to threaten him with public acknowledgment of your friendship. If he has read the appropriate chapter of our little handbook, he will immediately perceive the danger and withdraw from whatever nefarious activity you have caught him at.

Similarly, politicians in the cabinet may be dealt with according to the principles outlined in our chapter on cabinet officers. Let them carry the legislative ball to Capitol Hill. Keep them testifying before the committees. Send them on inspection tours of Vietnam and the Middle East. Four years of this and you can get re-elected by running against your own cabinet.

The millionaires are a somewhat different matter. Money is always convenient and sometimes essential, which is why you appointed them in the first place. We can only hope that your particular millionaires are scions of great wealth and not self-made men. The man of inherited wealth is normally easily dealt with. He is never quite sure that he has accomplished anything worthwhile because of personal merit—it may all be attributable to his privileged condition in life. He is continually comparing his own modest achievements with those of men who started from scratch and accomplished at least as much. The self-made millionaire is an entirely different breed. John Kennedy once observed that nothing so strengthens a man's self-confidence as being elected President of the United States. Next to that, there is little which so strengthens a man's self-esteem as amassing a few million dollars. The man who does is a hard man to put down. Once he finds out what a cabinet post really amounts to, he is extremely likely to make loud noises in the press, or resign at the worst possible moment, or both. Your only real defense against this type of personality is to let him live on expectations. Let him come to understand —most privately—that you are not especially pleased by the performance of your Vice President. Get the National Committee to examine the possible consequences of a campaign with him in the number-two spot, and so forth.

This is not, however, a sure-fire defense. Calvin Coolidge used the technique against his Secretary of Commerce, who'd become enormously rich as a mining engineer in the Orient, but Herbert Hoover made it to the White House and historians still debate whether Coolidge really had any choice when he decided not to seek re-election.

The wisest thing, Mr. President, is to avoid self-made men.

The intellectuals in the cabinet are to be dealt with by much the same methods used for speech writers. Their motives are similar and their notions of power equally naïve. Whenever possible, try to help the cabinet intellectual win the game of Who Talked to the President Last? This is all he really demands, and he will not really care if you listen. Just don't let him take notes.

Try Not to Antagonize the Career Civil Service

THE OFFICIAL SEAL of the Civil Service Commission bears the motto PALMAM QUI MERUIT FERAT which, I'm told on good authority, translates as "Let him who has deserved it bear the palm." It does not refer, Mr. President, to people who've won elections. Not even you.

President Truman remarks in his memoirs:

"The difficulty with many career officials in the government is that they regard themselves as the men who really make policy and run the government. They look upon the elected officials as just temporary occupants. Every President in our history has been faced with this problem: how to prevent career men from circumventing presidential policy." He fails to add that every President in history has lost the battle.

The problem lies in that second article of the Constitution from which you derive your powers, Mr. President. Look again at section two of that article. It says:

> He [i.e., you] shall have Power, by and with the Advice and Consent of the Senate, to make Treaties, provided two thirds of the Senators present concur; and he shall nominate, and by and with the Advice and Consent of the Senate, shall appoint Ambassadors, other public Ministers and Consuls, Judges of the Supreme Court, and all other Officers of the United States, whose Appointments are not herein otherwise provided for, and which shall be established by Law: but the Congress may by Law vest the Appointment of such inferior Officers, as they think proper, in the President alone, in the Courts of Law, or in the Heads of Departments.

The career Civil Service ignores practically everything in this section except the line reading "but the Congress may by Law vest the Appointment of such inferior Officers, as they think proper, in the President alone, in the Courts of Law, or in the Heads of Departments." You will find that over the years they have used this provision so effec-

tively that you cannot really control, or even greatly influence, the federal bureaucracy. You have a few hundred
jobs at the top to play with, but that's about all. And time is
against you.

You can, to a limited extent, intimidate them through
the Civil Service Commission. The Commissioner is your
appointee, placing him—as one of my former colleagues
once suggested—in the position of being the local Baptist
preacher while trying at the same time to run the whore-
house down the block. It is extremely hard to do both jobs
at the same time. But that's *his* problem. After all, he ac-
cepted the appointment, didn't he?

You use your Commissioner, Mr. President, to maneuver individual senior civil servants into untenable posi-
tions. Either they go along, or they get promoted. Promoted into super-grade jobs exempt from Civil Service protection and from which they can actually be fired. They
are under no compulsion to accept such promotions, of
course but if the alternative is several years studying oil
pipelines in Alaska or bringing peace to Indochina enough
of them will want to stay in Washington to give you the
outward appearance of being in charge.

But in the end, Mr. President, you can't win. And,
frankly, I'm not sure you should. At the beginning of this
little tome, I referred to the senior civil servant as a great
granite rock watching the rest of us come and go while
refusing to become swept up in the turbulence of our
enthusiasms. I even suggested that this might not necessarily
be bad for the country. Once, after many months of work-

ing with him and over a two-martini lunch, I finally summoned the courage to ask my senior career colleague in the office of the Secretary of Defense what, if any, his personal politics might be.

"I'm an aggressive neutral," he replied. "I hate you both."

Is it possible, Mr. President, that he was right?